Have you ever picked up a book, flipped to the dedication, and found that the author has dedicated a book to someone else and not to you?

Not this time.

For all those who dare to dream, do the work, and are willing to get a little uncomfortable in the process....this one's for you.

Table of Contents

Acknowledgments

If I were to acknowledge individually all the people who helped make Just Another Leap possible, I'd need to write three more chapters. My deepest gratitude for your wisdom, support and encouragement.

To Harika, Caleb, and the rest of the TEDxUMKC team: I will be forever grateful for the invitation to speak at TEDxUMKC! You started the ball rolling. Thanks to you I found comfort zones I didn't even know I had!

My thanks go to my parents, Charles and Anna Mae, who always believed in me. I miss you every day and really appreciate the signs that let me know you're right here with me.

To my brothers, Steve and Craig, and my sister-in-law, Linda, who have always been there for me, I appreciate you so much. Ours is a special family, and I am blessed to be a Layman. The after-dinner conversations are an added bonus.

Thanks to my closest friends. You have contributed to who I have become. I thank you for being yourselves, allowing me to do the same, and especially for loving me despite my flaws.

I also want to say thank you to my tribe. You exemplify the true meaning of a super connector. It's an honor to be in your circle of influence. I'd trust you with my proxy anytime!

To my professional team: I want to thank Jennifer, in her infinite wisdom, for putting The Book page on my website. If it weren't for you, Just Another Leap would still be on my "to do in the near future" list. To Wayne and Amy, thank you for taking my words and helping me put them on paper, and thank you, Cory, for your brilliance creating the cover.

Lastly, to everyone who has ever contributed to my leaps, thank you! No matter how difficult or overwhelming they felt at the time, they taught me valuable lessons, and pushed my belief of what's possible farther than I ever imagined.

Introduction

Have you ever walked into a bathroom and noticed that the toilet paper was on the roll backwards? Did it make you uncomfortable enough to change it? Whether it's an experience as significant as the exponential rate of change in business, dealing with the challenges of being a Sandwich Generation adult, or as small as a change in your workout routine, or that pesky toilet paper roll, all have the ability to push your comfort zones.

Dealing with change = Pushing comfort zones = Just another leap

Getting out of your comfort zones, whether by choice or not, can push you to accomplish things you never thought you could. Leaps are the moves you make to push your comfort zones as you go after your goals and dreams. Any leap, small or huge, intentional or not, is all about moving beyond your comfort zones.

"Just another leap" refers to pushing the next comfort zone, and the next and the next. This book is designed to take the fear out of taking the leap and introduces the process that will get you from there to here, both in business and in your personal life. It also helps you cultivate the proper mindset, because ultimately, it's not what happens to you, but your mindset towards any type of change and how you respond, that will determine how successful you are in your leap.

We have to continue to ask ourselves if the fear of the unknown is keeping us from taking the action that will move us forward and help us make the impact we want to make in the world. In his book *Drive: The Surprising Truth about What Motivates Us*, Daniel Pink says, "We need a place of productive discomfort. "If you're too comfortable, you're not productive. And if you're too uncomfortable, you're not productive. Like Goldilocks, we can't be too hot or too cold." In this book, you'll learn how to find that place of productive discomfort.

We're all different, so there isn't one way to take leaps that works for everyone every time. *Just Another Leap* is about the process. You can apply it to whatever area of your life you're looking to change. This book isn't meant to be comprehensive, but offers a practical guide and a place to start.

This book can't help those who are stuck and like it that way no matter the cost. It's intended for folks who are faced with change, whether it's by intent or something that's outside their control. It's also for those seeking something in their life but they're not quite sure how to define it, and once they define it, they're unsure how to get it.

Change is hard, so I keep things simple by sharing in layman's terms (hey, it's my name—it comes easy to me!). Some of the information may be familiar, but you'll also discover new insights. Choosing to act on it is up to you.

In the book, you'll hear more of my story as well as the stories of other people who have all had their own "there to here" journey:

- Congenital amputee and ESPY award winner Kyle Maynard
- Real estate mogul Barbara Corcoran
- Spanx founder Sara Blakely
- Wife and mother Mindy Hager
- Robohand creator Richard Van As

This book is as much for organizations as it is for individuals. For organizations to successfully navigate change, they can't continue to do what they've always done. Organizations that are risk adverse choose to stay in their comfort zone. But to stay relevant in today's marketplace, organizations have to be willing to take risks and push comfort zones. They have to go beyond the typical managerial-driven approach to business that encompasses planning, budgeting, organizing, etc. There's an old saying, "the fish stinks from the head." When it comes to change, there's no truer phrase, because it starts with leadership.

Even in an organization, it appears the problem lies in shifting the *individual's* outlook on change within the organization. In fact, independent studies at Harvard University and the London Business School revealed that "over 70% of all change initiatives in corporations do not deliver the required results" and "the most common cause of failure . . . insufficient focus on people."[1]

Organizational culture is an unseen force that's shaped by each individual's attitudes, habits, and beliefs. It starts with putting the right people in the right positions. Then, empowering everyone in the organization to take their own leaps and achieve goals helps to gain their buy-in during the change process, helping the organization achieve success.

> ❝ *Change the way you look at things,*
> *and the things you look at change.* ❞
>
> —**Wayne Dyer**

Dealing successfully with any type of change means having an insatiable curiosity, being able to look beyond your current box, and embracing risk and the potential discomfort of failure. You must have a willingness to be uncomfortable, if only for a moment, because this is how we progress. No worthwhile aspiration can be accomplished from within our comfort zone. Only in giving up the security of what we know can we create new opportunity, build our ability, grow influence, and ultimately change our lives.

It all starts with a decision!

ONE

You Don't Have to Vault the Entire Staircase

❝Faith is taking the first step even when you don't see the whole staircase.❞

—Martin Luther King

From there to here: It's a fascinating journey. For some, it's smooth; for others, it's extremely rocky. We often think we have to vault the entire staircase, but we don't know how. Here's the key: It's not about taking the whole staircase in one shot. You just have to make the decision to move forward, and take the first step in faith.

When we focus on where we are ultimately trying to end up, rather than just the step in front of us, it can be paralyzing. Here's just one example of how this can happen. I was out cycling one Saturday morning in July. It was getting hotter by the second, so I decided to take a shortcut. Taking the shortcut meant going over a hill that was a killer combination of long and steep, but I was in good shape and cycled regularly so I figured I could handle it. Plus, if I could tackle this hill, it would cut 30 minutes off the time it would take me to get home, so I started climbing. Cars full of parents and kids passed me at a steady rate on their way to the ball diamonds at the top. With each pedal stroke I kept my focus on the top of the hill. Suddenly, about three quarters of the way up, I thought, "I can't do this." My body immediately responded and I had to unclip my shoes from my pedals, plant my feet, and hope I didn't slip on the asphalt. Then came the long walk of shame to the top. I suspect the people passing me were wondering, "Who is this chick and why is she walking her bike?!" It was then that I realized I had talked myself out of the climb. If I had continued to believe I could do it, and focused on the ground just in front of my handlebars, the top of the hill wouldn't have seemed so far away. All I needed to do was focus on the immediate task at hand instead of worrying about how much further I had to go.

Many of us, when we see a big obstacle in front of us, don't even want to attempt it, because it's just too big and we can't even fathom how we're going to make it work. We start looking at that entire staircase, and we don't know exactly how to reach the top; we just know we need to make a change. Once we know we want to make a change, we just need to take it one step at a time. Just like when we're climbing a steep hill, we need to start with the goal but focus on the individual steps.

We need to approach it this way because we're hardwired to resist change. This is something that is in our internal makeup from the hunter-gatherer days, when change meant danger. So even now, when we try to take on too much, it can become overwhelming, and we find ourselves procrastinating—also known as creatively avoiding taking action—because our brain is trying to help us avoid danger.

When making any type of change, it literally starts with the first step. With the first step, you're making a decision to change.

> *Every human has four endowments—self-awareness, conscience, independent will, and creative imagination. These give us the ultimate human freedom . . . The power to choose, to respond, to change.*
>
> -Stephen Covey

The Importance of That First Single Decision

You're where you are today because of decisions that you've made, and if you're going to make changes in your life, once again, you need to start with a decision. We tend to muddy the situation with so many decisions that we get stuck. We keep thinking about all the different things we need to do to achieve more in our life and in our business, but we can really make our lives much happier by just focusing on the single decision that can move us forward.

The decision doesn't have to be a big one to have a big impact, and it doesn't always have to be something big that leads to the decision. Sometimes, it can just be a subtle nudge, but you have to be listening in order to catch it.
For an organization, the leader must drive the decision initiative, because the only way the culture has a chance to truly shift is by starting at the top and working down. Then, one decision builds on the next and it just keeps going.

" Start where you are. Use what you have.
Do what you can. "

Start Where You Are

Before you make any decisions that will help you get where you want to go, consider starting with a big-picture view.

First, take a look at where you are now. Too often, we try to internalize these ideas or just think about them without putting anything down on paper. Getting it on paper can be really useful to create new awareness and live intentionally instead of by accident. Take the time to look at the different areas in your life from a 30,000-foot view: career/business, finances, health, family/marriage, relationships, time, leisure, personal growth, peace of mind, etc.

Ask yourself, "Where am I today? If I rated each on a scale of 1 to 10, with 1 being the worst and 10 being the best it possibly can be, where does each area fall on the line?"

Career/business	1_____	10
Finances	1_____	10
Health	1_____	10
Family/marriage	1_____	10
Relationships	1_____	10
Time	1_____	10
Leisure	1_____	10
Personal growth	1_____	10
Peace of mind	1_____	10

Once you take that 30,000-foot view of what's going on in your life, you can consider what you want the end result to look like, and what you need to do to get there. What does ultimate success look like in your life? Fast forward to yourself at 80 years of age. Now look back. What have you accomplished?

This isn't just about monetary wealth; it's about success and significance. Look at the accomplishments in your business life and your personal life:

- Who's there with you on the journey?
- What challenges have you overcome?
- Who have you become in the process?
- Coming back to the present day, are you on track to make it a reality?

You take a look at the overall picture, and then you take a particular area and break it down so you can go into more depth on what you want to achieve in each area.

This may seem like a lot of work, but remember, the best coaches don't give you the answers; they ask questions to help you find your answers. This process will help you uncover the answers that lie within.

My big aha recently regarding my health was that I needed to stop doing only high-intensity exercise. I had been so stuck in my habits and just doing what I thought was best for me that I completely missed the fact that it was too much for my body. Once I recognized how much the high-intensity workouts were hurting, I stepped back to look at the bigger view and decided to incorporate yoga into my exercise routine.

Take a step back and really look at what's going on, and if something isn't right, whether it's in your business or your personal life, determine the pain, frustration, or stress you're experiencing as a result of what's happening. That will help you pinpoint the first decision or first step you can make to get back on track.

Remember, the first step doesn't have to be a big thing. It's the continuous movement forward that makes the difference.

These are big questions to ponder, but they will help you determine if you're happy, unhappy, or want to make a change but don't know how. You may also find out you're stuck and like it. If things aren't going the way you want, there has to be a point in your life and in your business where you say, "I choose something different" or "Something has got to change." Without that trigger, nothing will ever change.

This happened to me a number of years ago. In 2001, I was in a sales position that I absolutely loved. I had a horse that I showed and I was at the barn riding three to four days a week; I could also tell you what was on television every night of the week. I had great friends and family and everything that goes with it. But something was just missing.

A big aha moment happened when my friend Merry Ann, whom I had known for eight years, was tragically killed in a car accident. Merry Ann was an extraordinary individual and touched so many lives in a positive way. There were so many people at her memorial service that they had to open all the doors to allow room for the overflowing crowds.

I remember sitting in the chapel thinking, "I want to be remembered for making a difference." For me, that was a light switch that I flipped, and I had no idea where it was going to lead me. Looking back, I now know that it was the catalyst that eventually led me where I am today.

It's a common theme. Something happens in our life that's very dramatic, like a heart attack, or it's that subtle nudge that for some reason hits us just so and we say, "I am on the wrong path. I need to make a change." Or we're thrown into a situation, such as suddenly having to deal with an ailing parent, and have to make it work.

Sometimes, the decision can come from pure frustration, when you can't stand being in a situation one more minute. The crap can actually be a huge motivator. Sometimes, it's a toxic relationship or maybe a caustic business environment that you're in. So, you need to identify what's causing the frustration, and then once you've internalized that and say that you're ready to move forward, you're on your path.

Some questions to ponder when you're looking for clarity about what needs to change:
- What's working?
- What's not working?
- What do you feel you want to or need to change in your life?
- What do you feel you want to or need to change in your business?
- What are you willing to give up in order to make the change?
- Will you actually do the work to make it happen?

> ❝ *The greatest accomplishment began as a decision once made and often a difficult one.* ❞
>
> -Michael Rawls

Conscious Decision Making

First, come up with a plan ahead of time so you are being proactive instead of having to react in the instant you need to make a decision. I like the 10-10-10 method from Suzy Welch: When confronted with a decision, think through what it would feel like 10 minutes, 10 months, and 10 years from now. This will help give you perspective on how important the decision is.

Write down the pros and cons so you can actually see the potential results of the decision. There's power in putting it on paper. If you have to make a quick decision, then do this in your head. Also consider the positive future benefits for the decision you make.

Ask others to support you. When I have a big decision to make, I call on my team—my close circle, my advisers, who I have asked to hold me accountable and to call me on my "stuff" when needed. They come from different industries, different walks of life. They don't tell me what to do, but they ask enough questions to help guide me down the path to my own decision, just like a good coach would.

Finally, just do it! Too often we delay making a decision because we're afraid of making the wrong decision. But remember, the majority of wrong decisions can be corrected. Consider the cost of delaying a decision versus the cost of making a wrong decision. When I need to make a decision but I have not yet chosen the exact course I'm going to take, that's the most uncomfortable place to be. Staying stuck doesn't always feel good; sometimes, if you can just move a little bit, things start happening. The subconscious kicks in, and that's when you start to notice opportunities, information, resources, and so on. It comes from just a little bit of movement. Just go with your gut and, later, pivot if needed.

> *Success does not consist in never making mistakes but in never making the same one a second time.*

-George Bernard Shaw

Those Darn Cosmic 2 x 4s

Sometimes, if we don't learn our lesson from a painful experience, we find ourselves reliving the same experience again (and again). I call this a cosmic 2 x 4. Cosmic 2 x 4s come in a variety of shapes and sizes.

I experienced a lot of 2 x 4s around relationships. I would go from one relationship to another, and whether it was two months or two years later, it would be a different guy but a similar story. Each time, I'd think that time and age had made me a different person, but I would end up in yet another relationship that ended up being the same. Instead of taking the time to really reflect, I made decisions out of fear. That cosmic 2 x 4 would smack me upside the head, until I finally learned the lesson.

People do this in business too. They continually choose to stay with what they know, even if it's costing them financially. It's always easier to see from the outside looking in; you see them making decisions that really don't make sense for the success of the business, but they're stuck in the habitual and stay there even though they're getting whacked with that 2 x 4.

> *Every excuse I ever heard made perfect sense to the person who made it.*

-Dr. Daniel T. Drubin

The Benefits of a Post-Mortem

The cosmic 2 x 4 shows up when you don't take time to learn from your experiences. A post-mortem can speed up the learning process so you can avoid future 2 x 4s. The post-mortem is all about what went wrong, so you can figure out why you didn't get the job or why things didn't work out the way you hoped—and do things differently the next time.

Between relationships, I hadn't stopped long enough to do a post-mortem on the previous relationship to say what worked and what didn't. I couldn't clearly see the situation when I was in the middle of it. Eventually, I said, "I'm done; I'm ready for something to change." And when I stepped back to learn from those relationships, I realized that the connecting feature was me. It was my mindset, what I was willing to put up with.

It wasn't until I did a post-mortem, and through that awareness and reflection got to the other side, that I realized how badly I was stuck. It took time to acknowledge where I needed to grow as a person. I also needed to ask myself what kind of person I wanted in my life, and what qualities that person would have, in order to make better choices going forward.

Accountability is a huge piece of the post-mortem. It's easy to blame somebody or something else for where you are in life or the results you're getting, but with the post-mortem you can start to recognize the ways you've contributed to the situation. Even though each partner had his faults, I saw that I had accountability in each relationship and I'm far from perfect myself. It's not easy to truly become accountable and ask yourself, "What did I contribute?" But sometimes, you have to say, "I'm wrong," and be willing to face it and fix it.

When you truly sit back and reflect on what decisions you've made, what worked, what didn't, and what kept you off track, it can help put you back in your power. It can help make your path a little bit easier the next time. And it's a powerful thing when you can finally say, "I'm not going to do that anymore because that really hurts." That's when you start living intentionally instead of by accident.

> *It is not only what we do, but also what we do not do,*
> *for which we are accountable.*
>
> -Molière

I recommend post-mortems to my corporate clients too.

Do a post-mortem about situations in your business and ask:
- **How did things go?**
- **What didn't go as well as I/we wanted it to?**
- **Do I/we keep doing what's always been done, or challenge what I/we think I/we know and try new approaches to problems?**
- **Do I/we proactively seek new challenges or just manage those I/we already have?**
- **How can I/we make it better the next time, if given the opportunity?**

A post-mortem doesn't have to take hours; it can even be just jotting down some quick notes about what you've learned.

After I give a keynote, I take some notes and ask myself, "What were the stories or information where I got the best feedback or the best laughter? What didn't quite sink in and how can I tweak things to do it better the next time?"

It's always about doing it just a little bit better. It doesn't have to be dramatic; just take those little steps.

Some of the most successful people on the planet regularly evaluate their performance; in fact, it's how they got to that level in the first place. The top athletes in any sport are constantly asking themselves, "What do I need to do differently?" The greatest leaders of our time are willing to ask, "What does our organization need to do differently to be better?" and of their team, "What do you think?"

This is so effective because the faster you have the awareness, the faster you can move to the next level. Otherwise, you just stay stuck.

❝You can't connect the dots looking forward; you can only connect them looking backwards. So you have to trust that the dots will somehow connect in your future. You have to trust in something—your gut, destiny, life, karma, whatever. Because believing that the dots will connect down the road will give you the confidence to follow your heart even when it leads you off the well-worn path; and that will make all the difference.❞

—Steve Jobs, Stanford commencement speech, June 2005

Reality-Check Your Decision

Of course there are a lot of things that will have to happen to reach your goals, but don't talk yourself out of the hill like I did; just focus on taking one step, then the next and the next. With each step, you'll get more comfortable and gain confidence as you continue to move forward.

Now that you've made your decision, look at what outcome it is attached to. Is it your bigger vision? Maybe it's one of your big business goals that you've set for the year. It could also be an internal shift like what I experienced after my friend Merry Ann passed away.

Once you become aware of what it is that you want to do, achieve, or be, then you need to ask yourself, is this decision going to get me closer to, or take me off track from, the outcome that I'm looking for? If you realize your decision is going to take you off track, then stop, reassess, and find another way forward. If you're still unclear about what outcome you want, the next chapter will help you figure out your "why."

... Insert brownie break here ... mmm...

TWO
Start with Y ... or Maybe Z

> 66 *The two most important days in your life are the day*
> *you are born and the day you find out why.* 99
>
> -Mark Twain

It's hard to believe, because I have done a complete 180 and now try to do everything I can to improve my health, but when I was in my twenties and mid-thirties, I used to smoke a pack of cigarettes a day.

George Burns could smoke cigars until he was in his nineties, but smoking seriously affected my health. In fact, when I was in my twenties, my doctor told me that for the number of times I had bronchitis, I was well on my way to having emphysema, and I should stop smoking immediately.

Not being health conscious, I just didn't see that it was going to be a problem, and I kept smoking even though it was a detriment to my health. I had blinders on—until I finally got sick of being sick all the time.

So I met a friend for dinner. We had a glass of champagne. I smoked one last cigarette and she did, too, because we were both planning on quitting—and that was the last cigarette I had in my life. My friend started up again two weeks later, but I was beyond done.

Recognizing that I was sick of being sick allowed me to make that shift in my mind that was necessary in order to quit. I've heard similar stories from other former smokers. I've learned that having a powerful "why" is the key; it's what's going to help you achieve what you want in life.

Your "why" is the vision and values that drive you.

It's your personal philosophy that guides your life and the decisions you make. When you have that "why," it helps you overcome the greatest obstacles as well as your greatest fears.

Decide upon your major definite purpose in life and then organize your actions around it.

-Brian Tracy

Pigeons and Our Decisions

In the late '60s, psychiatrist George Ainslie was doing research on pigeon behavior, and he noticed a funny thing about how pigeons make decisions. This observation led to his identifying a tendency called hyberbolic discounting, which humans also have. In layman's terms, hyperbolic discounting means that our subconscious has a reward-processing center, and we're able to stay focused on the greater reward until there's a small reward right in front of us, which distracts us from the greater reward. The "why" is what helps us stay focused on the greater reward.

In my case with quitting smoking, I had to stay focused on my "why," which was to be healthy again, instead of allowing myself to have a cigarette in the moment. And it's no different than when you want to lose weight but are tempted by a donut or you want to grow your business but cold calls are the last thing you want to do.

But when you know and understand your "why," then you can stay focused on the greater reward and move forward. (This works equally well for both business and personal goals.)

LEAP EXERCISE

Do you recall the last time you gave in to the smaller reward instead of staying focused on the greater reward? Was there an emotional payoff (either positive or negative) attached to it?

The only person you are destined to become is the person you decide to be.

-Ralph Waldo Emerson

The Fire in Your Belly

Some of the most successful people in the world have overcome extraordinary adversity; determination is what kept them going no matter what challenges they encountered. No matter what happened, they knew they would figure out a way to get through any hardship and accomplish their goal.

Determination, or inner drive, or fire in the belly, can range from simply enjoying the path to what some would consider "a little crazy," a ruthless obsession for achieving their end result. Jack Dorsey, co-founder of Twitter and founder of Square, is the perfect example of this. Growing up in St. Louis, Jack loved maps and trains and listening to the chatter of the emergency dispatch center. He noticed how everyone would share updates in short bursts, and this observation eventually led to the idea for Twitter. From those early beginnings, he became obsessed with taking what we do in real life and creating virtual spaces that mimic that behavior.

When you see what other people have accomplished, it reminds you of what's possible when you're determined.

I've had the honor to meet two amazing athletes who have shown tremendous determination, and I think you'll find their stories inspiring.

Kyle Maynard[2] was born a congenital amputee. His arms end at the elbows and his legs at the knees, and he stands just four feet tall. Kyle battled against the odds to become one of the top high school wrestlers in the state of Georgia. In 2005, he broke the world record in the modified bench press by lifting 360 pounds, which was three times his body weight. Kyle is also an ESPY Award–winning mixed martial arts athlete, and on January 15, 2012, he became the first quadruple amputee to climb Mount Kilimanjaro without assistance; he crawled all 19,340 feet in just 10 days. His next goal is to climb Mt. Aconcagua in 2015. At 22,840 feet, Aconcagua is the highest mountain in South America. This will be Kyle's second of the Seven Summits (the highest peaks on each continent). Kyle is a keynote speaker and author of the book *No Excuses*, a theme which he lives each and every day.

Nikki Stone[3] competed in the 1998 Winter Olympics in Nagano, Japan, and became America's first-ever Olympic champion in the sport of inverted aerials. In aerial skiing, athletes approach a 10-foot snow jump at approximately 40 miles per hour, flip and/or twist to a height of 50 feet, and land on a 45-degree hill. What made Nikki's performance at Nagano so unbelievable was the fact that less than two years earlier, a chronic injury prevented her from standing, much less walking or skiing down a slope at almost 40 miles per hour, and doctors believed she would never jump again.

Even if you're an introvert or a wallflower (like I used to be), you can become a more determined person; you don't have to change your personality. You can start by practicing these strategies: become more focused, have a strong sense of direction, don't take no for an answer (be persistent, not annoying), and become better at saying what you do and don't like. And finally, finish what you start. Some people's determination is fueled by a passion for finishing what they started; they can't stand the idea of leaving something half-done.

> **"**Inaction breeds doubt and fear. Action breeds confidence and courage. If you want to conquer fear, do not sit home and think about it.
> Go out and get busy.**"**
>
> -Dale Carnegie

Do It Anyway

"Do it anyway" sounds easy enough, but fear stops many people from actually going after their big goals. I know, because I used to be one of them.

People who knew me when I wasn't so bold ask, "How did you start keynote speaking? How did you get bold enough to ask that question? How did you reach out to somebody you didn't know on social media?" The truth is, one action led to another. Not all were successful, but they gave me courage. On occasion I took a huge leap of faith and really threw myself out there, and it increased my confidence for the next leap.

My new motto is, "Do something bold every day." Bold has different meanings to different people. For example, you won't find me being bold by bungee jumping off a bridge, but I will reach out to the CEO of a company when looking to make an introduction.

What does bold look like to you?

We hesitate to be bold because we tend to create a bigger (negative) story than the reality. What we imagine in our minds is often much worse than what could actually happen. So it's really in knowing the difference. When you face what scares you, ask yourself, "What is the worst that could *actually* happen? Would it really be that bad?"

If you're thinking, "I don't have the right education," "I don't have a plan," "I don't know how to take the first step," or maybe "I don't deserve to take the first step," just take the first step. Even if you don't know how or think you don't deserve it, start moving forward.

That's what I did. I was in a position where I was introducing speakers, organizing events, and leading a team in Kansas City. I knew I wanted to speak, but I was scared of speaking and I wasn't quite sure how I was going to do that. I watched the speakers and admired them. Some of them were highly trained professionals, and others had just kind of fallen into it, yet they found their passion and hit their stride.

For me, it wasn't a matter of saying, "I want to be a keynote speaker and I'm going to go to school for this," but the desire was there. I kept watching, and opportunities would happen. I just kept saying yes and I ended up with the next step and the next step and the next step, to the point where I chose to throw myself out there and say, "Yes, I speak" when I really didn't, which gave me an extraordinary opportunity, and then I gained the knowledge as I was going down the path.

I've wondered numerous times where I would be in my career today had I not said yes. I am great at saying yes now. When you're getting overwhelmed, there are times that you need to learn not to say yes, so you don't get overextended, but always say yes to opportunities that will take you further down the right path. Remember that your path might not look like anyone else's path. It's important to let go of the "have tos" others might impose on you; don't let their opinions or advice carry over into your own negative self-talk. Decide what's best for you.

I've learned from all the experiences I've had, and all the knowledge I've gained over the years has gotten me to where I am now. In my younger days I wasn't good at goal setting. I was more of a go-with-the-flow kind of person and it showed in the results I obtained. Now, I do plan and set goals regularly. I have a firm route that I take, but I'm also flexible and know that pivots are sometimes necessary.

I know how much more you can accomplish when you set goals, keep looking up, and look for bigger things even though you may not have the resources, or even what you feel are the skills, to get there today. All you have to do is take the first step.

> ❝ *When you're up to your ass in alligators, sometimes it's hard to remember that your original objective was to drain the swamp.* ❞

Look Past the Alligators

It's all about where you place your focus. I love the quote above about alligators; when I'm working with leadership teams, I'll ask, "What are your alligators? What are you focusing on?" Bigger yet, "What else are you leaving out?"

They'll name all these things that are holding them back or are taking up time that they don't have. They start to recognize that the little stuff isn't necessarily helping to achieve their goals, yet they're getting mired in the muck, so to speak.

You do need to acknowledge the alligators, though. If you don't, you're going to get bit. But you can't focus on them, or you'll just get more of the same. So once you've acknowledged the alligators, your "why" helps you look up. You look past the alligators and head up the staircase; otherwise, you'll stay stuck in the swamp.

LEAP EXERCISE

What alligators are you facing right now in life? Personal or business, it doesn't matter, just write them down.

> ❝ *The best way to predict the future is to create it.* ❞
>
> -Peter Drucker

Sometimes you find yourself following someone else's "why," but that doesn't work so well. It's much more effective to follow your own passion, your own reason for moving forward. If you want to benefit from your own internal motivation, it's essential to go back to your "why."

In fact, if you lack confidence and start comparing yourself to others, this can de-motivate you. For example, *SUCCESS* magazine highlights such a wide variety of extraordinary stories that it's easy for some to get caught up in thinking, "I could never accomplish what they have. Look at the obstacles they overcame; I don't have those resources."

But the common thing is that each of those successful people has their own "why," just like you have yours. Remember that you have a unique story that only you were meant to live. Stop looking at other's "whys" and stay focused on your own. We don't all find our "why" at the same stage in our lives, but it happens faster when we're looking for it.

I am a huge fan of Simon Sinek. I first came across him when I saw his TED talk, where he talks about the power of "why." His golden circle diagram shows the Why, the What, and the How:

The Why: the driving motivation, like a cause or belief, that inspires you to act

The What: the tangible results from your principles in action, like proof that you're acting on your "why"

The How: the guiding principles or specific actions you take to make your "why" become a reality

As Simon explains, any business can explain *what* it does, and some can explain *how* they do it, but very few can clearly articulate *why* they do it.

The "why" isn't the money or the profit. It's not the product or service. It's the purpose for creating the company and it's at the core of everything.

For example, Sam Walton with Walmart: he wanted to make quality goods affordable and available to rural folks in the United States.

You've got Herb Kellerman with Southwest Airlines; he wanted to take stodginess out of air travel and bring it to the common people.

One of the most easily recognized stories is Bill Gates with Microsoft, who had a vision of accessible information for all.

They didn't get into the "what" or "how." They started with their "why." That's what drove each of their businesses.

It's worth spending some time to determine what your "why" is. If it doesn't come to you immediately, don't worry; it will. Just let it happen.

> ***If you don't decide what your life is about, it defaults to what you spend your days doing.*** **"**
>
> -Robert Brault

LEAP EXERCISE

Start to identify your "why" by answering the following questions. Just let the answers flow for now and you can corral them a little later. If you find yourself hesitating on some of the questions, go on to the next one. This exercise doesn't have to be done in one sitting. Relax.

- What's important to you? (e.g., personal growth, mental and physical well-being, taking on challenges, etc.)
- What are your values?
- Who has inspired you? What qualities do those folks have that you would also like to have?
- What do you love about your life? Your work? Your family, friends, and other relationships?
- When are you at your best? Your worst?
- What inner qualities would you like to adopt or improve about yourself?
- What big events impacted your life? Reflect on these big moments and the lessons you learned from them.
- If you had unlimited resources and time, what would you do?
- What do you want your legacy to be?

Be honest with yourself, and also allow yourself to dream past your current reality.

Once you've answered all the questions, go back and circle the words or phrases that really stand out and resonate at a core level. Use those words to create a "why" statement that's 1–2 paragraphs long. If it's easier just to keep the words in list form, then go with that. Remember, it's not permanent; as you evolve, your "why" will also evolve.

> ❝ To ask, 'How do you do it?' is already starting off on the wrong foot. When reaching for the stars, there does not have to be a 'how' if there is a big enough 'why'. ❞
>
> -Criss Jami

Knowing your why is extraordinarily powerful, but remember, nothing starts until you say yes. Google's executive chairman, Eric Schmidt, summed this up perfectly in his 2012 commencement address at the University of California at Berkeley:

"Find a way to say yes to things. Say yes to invitations to a new country. Say yes to meeting new friends. Say yes to learning a new language, picking up a new sport. Yes is how you get your first job, and your next job. Yes is how you find your spouse, and even your kids. Even if it's a bit edgy, a bit out of your comfort zone, saying yes means you will do something new, meet someone new and make a difference in your life, and likely in others' lives as well. … Yes is a tiny word that can do big things. Say it often."

Saying yes starts a chain reaction of progress. It pushes you out of your comfort zone. Connecting yes to your why fuels your determination and opens the door to new possibilities. What will you say yes to?

THREE

"Yes Buts,"
"What Ifs,"
and "I Don't Know How Tos"

❝If you realized how powerful your thoughts are, you would never think a negative thought.❞

-Peace Pilgrim

Here are just a few examples of the "yes buts," "what ifs," and "I don't know how tos" that keep us stuck. Have you ever heard yourself saying any of these?
"I'm a morning person."
"I don't do well at remembering names."
"Things don't work out for me."
"How can we? We've never done that before."
"There's never enough time."
"I can't think before that first cup of coffee."
"It's just one of those days."

Have you ever done something wrong and then played it over and over in your mind? *"How could I have been so stupid, why didn't I keep quiet, why didn't I say . . ."* This kind of self-talk is your negative thinking in action. And, oftentimes we don't just repeat it once or twice; we go on and on for weeks repeating that same conversation in our head.

As we are doing this, we are recording the event in our mind like it is happening again. And, as we dwell on the negative, this builds a belief of "how we are" (our normal) in that situation. (Have you ever heard yourself say, "Yeah, I can't help it; it's just how I am!")

❝When the student is ready, the teacher will appear.❞

-Zen proverb

Lightbulb Moments

I used to be a wallflower, and I was very uncomfortable in networking events. Now that I have reconnected with some friends whom I knew in high school, they're surprised to hear about my years as a wallflower; they say, "That wasn't like you in high school. We remember you as outgoing. How on earth did that happen?"

Here's what happened: a series of life experiences eroded my self-worth and self-esteem and put me in a shell. On some level I knew it was happening, but I wasn't quite sure how I was going to get out of it. I didn't know at the time that it was my own beliefs that were keeping me in that spot.

They say that when the student is ready, the teacher will appear, and that was certainly the case for me. At a networking event one day, I heard a woman speak. She was one of those people who lit up the room when she walked in. I remember looking at her and thinking to myself, "I don't know what that is, but I want some of that."

Back then, it was really outside my comfort zone to walk up and talk to somebody. But I did it anyway, and introduced myself to the speaker. I asked, "Where do I get more of this information?" and she said, "Well, I'm speaking on the same topic tomorrow for another group." The next day, I went to hear her speak on the very same topic. I was mesmerized, caught up in whatever it was that she had.

I talked to her again on the second day, and she suggested I go through a program that had made a significant impact on her life. It was an easy yes for me, and learning the concepts in the program, the lightbulb moments were so numerous it was like there were paparazzi in my head.

This program gave me the cognitive tools to finally understand how I created my limiting beliefs. I was more aware of what I was thinking. I knew why I had become a wallflower. I knew why I wasn't accomplishing everything that I wanted in my business. I had worked with coaches in the past and identified goals, but then I kept pulling back and wouldn't take the steps to accomplish it. I wasn't working to my potential. My eyes were now opened to new possibilities, and it was a huge turning point in my life.

I find that a lot of people have followed the same path. They appear to be outgoing people that others assume will be super successful, and then they go through a time when there's all this self-doubt and they start to question who they are. They get kind of lost.

Supermodels are a great example. We look at them and think, "Oh, my, she's drop-dead gorgeous," but there are plenty of people telling her she isn't good enough or thin enough or pretty enough, and she starts to believe it, which can be really damaging over time. It's just crazy the messages we receive in today's society. To change this and move forward, we eventually have to learn how to get out of our heads and out of our own way. Once we can do this, we're able to stop subconsciously sabotaging ourselves so we can achieve what we want in life.

> ❝ We cannot solve our problems with the same thinking we used when we created them. ❞
>
> -Albert Einstein

Thoughts, Thoughts, and More Thoughts

Every single person has these "yes buts," "what ifs," and "I don't know how tos." So how do we combat them? Start by being aware.

In the first two days of the mindset program I took, they talked about self-talk—that mind chatter that we all have. You can call it "monkey mind," or "head trash," or whatever you want, but the fact is we think more than 50,000 thoughts a day, and I've even heard it can be as many as 65,000; let's just say it's a lot of thoughts.

Whether we're saying them out loud, or thinking them to ourselves, or somebody says something to us, or we're reading an article, we're constantly taking in those thoughts. And our subconscious takes everything we think and say and stores it as fact. The mind is like a giant hard drive that's storing the information contained in all of our thoughts and never asking questions. We have to become aware of what we think and say because some of it is helping us and some of it is holding us back, and our subconscious can't tell the difference.

We often don't even realize where the negative thoughts are coming from, but in fact, negativity surrounds us. A UCLA study reported that the average one-year-old child hears the word *no* more than 400 times a day. Then add to that negative start all the beliefs we create based on our experiences and the messages we heard growing up.

Did you recall hearing any of these as a child?
"You are wonderful."
"Look at what you can do . . ."
"You can accomplish whatever you want."
"You are a bad child."
"You are no good at . . ."
"You will never amount to much."

Plus, we're being bombarded with negative messages every single day in the media. And if we're not aware, all of these negative messages are sinking in and affecting how we think, what we say, and what we believe, and we don't even know it.

In order to live intentionally instead of by accident, we have to cultivate an awareness of what we're thinking, what we're saying, what we're doing, and how we're functioning. We also need to recognize the impact of our words on those around us.

> ❛❛ *Tell the negative committee that meets inside your head to sit down and shut up.* ❜❜
>
> -Ann Bradford

Negativity Bias

To make things even worse, we're actually hardwired to focus on the negative. It helped our ancestors survive. When cavemen went out gathering food for their families, in order to survive they needed to be sharply aware of the possibility of attacks from saber-toothed cats hiding in the bush and be prepared to escape them. Even though in today's world we don't have a need to run from predators, an evolutionary imprint remains called the negativity bias.

The negativity bias means we tend to have greater sensitivity to negative events than to positive ones. Some researchers assume that, psychologically speaking, negative events weigh close to three times more than positive events, even if the negative events are relatively minor—the negatives can be as simple as our cell phone ringing or a boss that's overcritical, but they have more of an impact on us than positive events. In situations related to survival, a negativity bias is beneficial, but it can cause stress in everyday life. And, even worse, so much of the negativity we encounter is in our own subconscious thoughts, and we don't even realize it.

When you get stressed, you have a tendency to fall back into old thinking habits. The yes buts, what ifs, and I don't know how tos can multiply just like the alligators. You actually start to see more negative things when you focus on the negative rather than what's going right in your world.

The first thing is to become aware. Nothing will change until you do.

> *I'm continually trying to make choices that put me against my own comfort zone. As long as you're uncomfortable, it means you're growing.*
>
> -Ashton Kutcher

What's Normal?

Along with the yes buts, what ifs, I don't know how tos, and negativity bias, you also have your self-image, also known as your "normal"—how you know yourself to be. This normal is like a psychological thermostat that regulates your level of performance. Think about the climate control on your thermostat at home. Let's say it's summertime and the air-conditioning is set to 72 degrees. Anytime the room temperature begins to change, the thermostat sends a signal to the air conditioner to turn off or on in order to maintain the temperature at 72 degrees (its comfort zone). Anytime you go to make a change, or set a new goal, your "normal" attempts to keep you in your comfort zone. You don't consciously realize it, but you may feel it in the form of mental or physical discomfort. It may also show up in your performance.

Comfort zones can also be external. Have you ever accidentally ended up in the wrong part of town? Maybe you've walked into a restaurant or shop and immediately felt like you didn't belong there. Going to a networking event where you didn't know anyone can also be outside your comfort zone; it's a mental and physical sensation that you can feel, kind of like the toilet paper hanging on the roll the wrong way.

What we think about all day and what we expect, be it positive or negative, is our comfort zone.

Do one thing every day that scares you.

-Eleanor Roosevelt

LEAP EXERCISE

Expand Your Comfort Zones
Practice on the little things to help you deal with pushing bigger comfort zones. When you try these, pay attention to what it feels like to be uncomfortable.
- **Brush your teeth with the opposite hand.**
- **Put the toilet paper on the roll backwards (and leave it that way).**
- **Intentionally drive a different route to work and home.**
- **Try changing up your morning routine.**
- **Paint your nails/toenails a color that is NOT like you at all.**
- **Don't order the same coffee or breakfast you always do.**
- **Shift something in your typical routine at work.**

Now go a little bigger:
- **Say yes to something you have always wanted to do, but have been afraid to try for fear of failure, rejection, or embarrassment.**
- **Say no to something you really don't want to do, but are doing anyway out of guilt, fear, or shame.**

Your self-talk is the channel of behavior change.

-<u>Gino Norris</u>

Oh, Snap!

Here's a simple exercise that will help you start to identify your negative thoughts. It's especially helpful when you start to notice the comfort zones that are keeping you stuck. Wear a rubber band or bracelet on your wrist. When you catch yourself thinking something negative or even limiting, snap the band against your skin. Then, find a positive reframe for what you're thinking. (If you don't, the negative thought will be imprinted in your mind once again.) For example, if you find yourself saying or thinking, "I don't do well at remembering names," snap the band and say, "I'm getting better at remembering names." Or if you're thinking, "How can we? We've never done that before," identify the reasons you can do it: "We can learn it, we're willing to look at our options, we're capable of learning to do this, we can find an expert to guide us . . ."

Focusing on the positive instead of the negative is a new habit for most of us, and it takes time to create new habits. Use visuals to help you, such as a daily reminder on your cell phone. I also write on my bathroom mirror with an erasable marker when I am focusing on a new goal, or maybe there's a new quality in myself that I want to develop, or something I want to do. The note serves as a reminder every time I see it. I've also been known to use 3 x 5 cards and stick them on the visor in the car. Or you can use sticky notes.

The point is to have these little reminders to help keep us focused and on track as we're getting into new self-talk habits. More than 95 percent of what we do is controlled by our subconscious, so we have to become aware of these thinking habits that we have in order to change them.

Start by savoring the good stuff that happens to you. Studies from the field of neuroscience show that while negative events may be seared into your mind almost instantly, it takes 5–20 seconds to emotionally absorb a positive event. When something positive happens in your life, be sure to stop and take several moments to savor it. Visualize your positive experience with your senses; explore what you feel, hear, smell, touch, and see.

> ❝ Who are we but the stories we tell ourselves, about ourselves, and believe? ❞
>
> -Scott Turow

Chicken Coops and the Bogeyman

When you're put into a new situation or facing change, you may find yourself creating stories out of beliefs that may or may not be true. Stay aware so you can catch yourself in the cycle of the story. Do a reality check (this means stop making things up!) and tell a new story instead. Ask, Is this true? Is this *really* true, or am I embellishing a bit? Am I fearful? Is this something I can solve with a little help? What would that look like?

As kids, it's easy to create stories, but they can stick with us for years if we're not careful. When I was a kid, my grandparents lived on a farm in Lawrence, Kansas. When we stayed with them during the summer we helped with chores, one of which was getting eggs from the henhouse. There was a path to get to the henhouse, and there was a hedgerow between the house and the barnyard with an outbuilding on one side, so it was hard to see anything except what was on the path. One of my fears was that the bogeyman was going to jump out and get me while I was walking down that path, especially in the evening. As I got a little older, I recognized that this was a story I'd created, and I thought through what I'd been telling myself. First, who is the bogeyman? Why would he want me instead of the chickens or eggs? We're out in the country and it's a long drive from anywhere, so is it really worth his time to come all this way and wait just for me to walk through the barnyard? Besides, someone else would certainly see him, like the dog. By looking at the situation more logically, I was able to recognize there was nothing to fear.

> ❝ *Our job in this life is not to shape ourselves into some ideal we imagine we ought to be, but to find out who we already are and become it.* ❞
>
> -Steven Pressfield

Sometimes someone else's opinion or story has the ability to impact the stories you tell yourself for the rest of your life.

A woman I coached on a leadership team said when her son was in kindergarten, he was a bit of a class clown. One day, his teacher looked at him and said, "People don't like funny boys." She said her son is now in college and he still remembers that remark, and I'm sure it's impacting the way he shows up in the world.

As adults we still tell stories and let our self-talk take us down a negative path. Say, for example, you're at a networking event and you see a woman you've talked to previously. This time, she looks at you but doesn't acknowledge you. Immediately, you start to wonder why and imagine all the worst-case scenarios that probably aren't true.

What stories are you telling yourself that may or may not be true? Learning to dispute negative and limiting thoughts might take time and practice, but it is worth the effort. Once you start paying attention to your thinking, you'll probably be surprised by how much of it is inaccurate, exaggerated, or focused on the negatives of a situation.

It helps to have people around you help hold you accountable. Give them permission to correct you lovingly when they hear you saying something that's either limiting or negative. That "lovingly" is important; you don't want them to reach out and snap that rubber band on you. But do give them permission to point it out, because sometimes, we get stuck looking at the alligators, and if we're ever going to get out of the swamp, we need to be paying attention to what we're saying.

Sure, not every day will be positive, but you always have control over how you react to what's going on around you. You're entitled to have an occasional pity party as long as you follow two rules: don't stay long and don't invite anyone to join you. Either you get stuck in the yes buts and the negative self-talk, or, with self-awareness, you break out of it because you cannot take it for even one more second.

> *Every time you state what you want or believe, you're the first to hear it. It's a message to both you and others about what you think is possible. Don't put a ceiling on yourself.*
>
> -Oprah Winfrey

Dreaming big with my business and my personal goals keeps me moving forward and blocks out the negative self-talk. When I try to put a lid on what I think I can accomplish, then I shut down the opportunities that I see and what I believe is possible for me.

Another reason it's important to write new stories is because we tend to self-regulate so that we show up how we believe ourselves to be. For example, a student who typically gets Cs will scale things back if she gets an A, because she doesn't see herself as an A student. Or if you hit your sales goal halfway through the month, you may find yourself coasting the rest of the month instead of pushing to reach an even higher goal. Or if you're playing golf and you play a far better game on the front nine than you usually do, you will mess up on the back nine.

In the corporate environment, the self-regulation may show up in a different way. A leader who perceives the organization as running perfectly may not listen to others who have terrific ideas or come to them with a better way to do something. Add generational differences to the mix and it can create even more issues.

Remember, you get more of what you focus on and what you believe. Your mind will only perceive information that it's prepared to see.

Clarity gives you confidence during the process of changing something in your life. Focus on your strengths and gifts that transcend any specific job role/title that you've possessed. Reflect on those first and know you can grow. Confidence comes from a sense that you have a lot to offer— and you know what you have to offer, so remember that!

> **❝ *The beauty of the impostor syndrome is you vacillate between extreme egomania and a complete feeling of: 'I'm a fraud! Oh God, they're on to me! I'm a fraud!' So you just try to ride the egomania when it comes and enjoy it, and then slide through the idea of fraud.* ❞**
>
> -Tina Fey

Impostor Syndrome

Do any of these sound familiar?

"It was just luck."
"I'm not good enough."
"I never do anything right."
"I don't have a degree."
"Maybe I shouldn't have the success I have."

Impostor syndrome can make you feel like a giant phony.

Impostor syndrome means you focus on your shortcomings and failures—big and small—and let them crowd out your many accomplishments, so you end up attaching a pattern of wrongdoing to yourself. Fear of not being good or perfect enough can also stop you from taking that first step.

When impostor syndrome strikes, it's important that you know that it's your perception, but *not* necessarily reality. What you consider a "failure" needs to be put in appropriate perspective. You didn't do well in that job interview? That's okay; neither did thousands of other people. It's not personal. Remember, failures can lead to new, unforeseen opportunities!

You will learn that sometimes your best isn't good enough, but you are good enough. Failing at something means you failed, but it doesn't mean you are a failure.

Some of the most successful individuals in the world today didn't finish college, or what they're doing now has nothing to do with what they studied. Their success comes from the right mindset. The right attitude. The right self-talk. You can learn the skills, but following your passion, surrounding yourself with the right people, and having that insatiable curiosity to learn and grow is just as important, if not more important, than acquiring the necessary knowledge and skills.

> ❝ *We are what we repeatedly do. Excellence, then, is not an act, but a habit.* ❞
>
> -Aristotle

Triggers, Routines, and Rewards

As you create new goals, you'll be shifting comfort zones and creating new habits, because the old ones aren't working.

My friend Mindy's experience shows the impact of our self-talk, and how it can help us change our habits. Mindy was overweight and had been going to Weight Watchers for a long time, but the most she'd ever lost was seven pounds in a year. Then, before we had even met, she heard me speak at an event where I explained self-talk and how the stories that we have can keep us stuck.

After hearing me speak, she recognized that her self-talk was keeping her stuck. She had been judging herself based on how she'd done that week, and it kept her on a roller coaster where she never made any progress. She realized that she needed to make a mental decision to stick with it, and she decided that she was going to go to the gym every Saturday morning at 7 a.m. That way, the only thing she'd miss would be sleep. She was determined to follow the program and stick to her plan at all costs, no matter what the results.

Mindy recognized something else, too. She told me, "In my own mind, I knew I wanted to run. I'd been working out, doing some stuff at the gym, but running was a huge hurdle for me, and I didn't realize that I've told myself all the time that I can't run." She said that when she first started, she literally would run a block, then would have to walk for a while. But then she could go two blocks, then four blocks. Over a year and a half, she lost 75 pounds. Less than two years after she started running, she did a 5K, and a year and a half after that, she ran a half marathon.

Mindy's accomplishments have also helped her family change their beliefs of what is possible. They've changed their eating and lifestyle habits, and she finds it really satisfying that at the same time that she's making huge, scary changes and overcoming hurdles, she's also helping her kids.

She's also learned that tomorrow is a new day; even if things didn't go well today, she will move on and keep going.

In Mindy's story we can see the simple neurological loop at the core of every habit. Discovered by MIT researchers, the loop has three parts:
1. Cue/trigger: this powers the loop
2. Routine: what you do
3. Reward: what you crave

Research shows that when you keep the cue and reward the same, but shift the routine in the middle, you're able to form a new habit. Mindy did just that. She started with a mental decision that something was going to change. She created a cue: going to the gym at a time that didn't interfere with work or her kids.

The routine she created was to follow the Weight Watchers program at all costs and not let the results of the week influence her actions.

Hitting her mini goals along the way was her reward, along with losing the weight and feeling better. Crossing the finish line at the 5K and the half marathon were even bigger rewards that increased her craving to continue.

Mindy's story shows us that when we take control of our self-talk and change the habit loop, we can achieve extraordinary things!

Creating a new habit takes self-awareness, determination, effort, and a good plan. But the biggest factor in successfully creating a new habit is your belief that things can change and, in fact, get better. You have the choice to respond in a different way.

> ❝ *Once you understand that habits can change, you have the freedom and the responsibility to remake them . . . Once you understand that habits can be rebuilt, the power of habit becomes easier to grasp and the only option left is to get to work.* ❞
>
> -William James

"Blowing bubbles is easy enough for a kid to pull off. Try not to overthink it too much or you'll probably suck at it."

—Todd Siebers

FOUR
There Must Be a Pony in There Somewhere

> *A pessimist sees the difficulty in every opportunity; an optimist sees the opportunity in every difficulty.*
>
> -Winston Churchill

Every day, experiences provide obstacles and opportunities. Your results are truly all about how you choose to look at things.

One day, I was on a 40-mile bike ride in Kansas City, Missouri, with my friend Trish, and we started to approach a hill called Hospital Hill. I had done this ride before, so I knew what was coming. I looked at Trish and said, "That hill ahead is a bear." (Well, that's not actually what I said, but you get the gist, right?)

There were two guys cycling right next to us who overheard me, and one of them turned to me and said, "That's not a hill; that's an opportunity." We had a lot more opportunities that day; every time we got to the bottom of one, we'd say, "Here comes another opportunity."

There's an old joke that's another great example of the importance of perspective. The parents of twin five-year-old boys were worried that the boys had developed extreme personalities—one was a total pessimist and the other one was a total optimist—so they took them to a psychiatrist. The psychiatrist took the pessimist into a room that was stacked to the ceiling with brand-new toys, and the little boy burst into tears.

The psychiatrist asked, "Don't you want to play with the toys?"

"Yes," the boy replied, "but if I did, I'd only break them."

Then, the psychiatrist turned to the optimist, and in trying to dampen his outlook, he took him into a room that was piled to the ceiling with horse manure. Instead of the little boy getting upset, he started excitedly digging into the pile as hard and as fast as he could.

"What are you doing?" The psychiatrist was just as baffled as he was with the other boy.

"With all this manure, there must be a pony in there somewhere!"

Obstacles are only failures if you let them cause you to quit. If you choose to let them help you, it is merely information you can learn from. If you look at it this way, every situation is a learning experience—again, it is your attitude toward the experience. It is in meeting crisis with determination that we measure up to life and its challenges and develop tenacity and inner strength.

> **From challenge rises opportunity, and our attitude has always been one of finding a way to win.**
>
> -Perry Puccetti

Obstacles and Undergarments

As the examples above show, the same thing, whether it's toys or manure or a hill, can be seen as an obstacle or an opportunity, depending on how you look at it. In business, some people are really great at dealing with obstacles. This is because they are determined. They have that fire in the belly, so they refuse to listen to the negative voices that may be around them and keep their focus on the opportunity, not the obstacles.

A great example of this is the story of the undergarment company Spanx, founded by Sara Blakely in 2000. I assume women readers will know what Spanx are, and I recently learned that they now make Spanx T-shirts for men. Sara came up against an obstacle when she couldn't figure out what undergarments to wear under a pair of white pants. She had spent $98 on the pants, which was a lot of money for her at the time, so she was determined to find a way to wear them. Out of frustration, she cut the feet off a pair of pantyhose so she could wear the hose under the pants, and that was her aha moment.

It took a lot of time and effort to create a prototype and secure a patent, but soon after, she managed to land a meeting with a buyer at Neiman Marcus. She did her pitch in the ladies room: first she put on the famous white pants without Spanx, and then she put on the pants with Spanx. Spanx were in

Neiman Marcus within three weeks, and today, Spanx is a $250 million brand.

During the creation process, the only people Sara shared her idea with were the patent lawyers and the people she talked to in the garment industry. She recognized that ideas are very fragile, and she was afraid that if she shared her idea with well-meaning friends, she might be discouraged.

So many million-dollar ideas are squashed because people want to tell you how it is, especially people who have never done it before. They may mean well, but they're basing their advice on their reality and their experiences.

We often have powerful people in our lives who have an influence on us, whether it's a teacher, a coach, or a pastor, but we have to be careful with the wisdom they share with us. Sometimes, it is extraordinarily valuable and in our best interest, and other times, it's based on their experience and they're trying to talk us out of it because they don't want to see us get hurt the way they may have been.

So pay attention to where the advice is coming from, and don't let anyone squash your dream if you're determined to make it happen. If need be, get advice from several people, wise people with more experience than you on topics related to your dream.

> *The important thing is not to stop questioning. Curiosity has its own reason for existing.*
>
> -Albert Einstein

The Power of Insatiable Curiosity

Albert Einstein was known for his curiosity. In a letter to a friend that was quoted in his biography by Walter Isaacson, Einstein said, "People like you and me never grow old. We never cease to stand like curious children before the great mystery into which we were born."

This kind of curiosity continued throughout his life and contributed to much of his breakthrough discoveries. He continued asking questions and learning throughout his life, not because he was told to, but because he had to.

Great leaders are insatiably curious. They continue learning and advancing because they absolutely want to learn more. Innovation doesn't happen when you follow the status quo.

Question everything. Be willing to ask the questions no one else is asking.

As kids, we were always asking why, what makes this tick, how does this work. Unfortunately, I think that natural curiosity often gets drilled out of us at an early age if it isn't nurtured properly. As adults, we still need to be learning and growing constantly. When you're asking questions all the time, it actually shifts your subconscious, because you start seeing things that you might otherwise have missed, and you get more excited to take leaps.

Insatiably curious people are, in a sense, seekers. They not only enjoy new experiences, but actively look for challenges that will stretch them, whether that involves making new friendships, learning new skills, or pushing themselves to do their best work.

As an example, my business partner calls me a master at connecting. I always seem to be in the right place at the right time and can make amazing connections even while waiting for an oil change on my car. That's because I have an insatiable interest to meet new people and am willing to ask questions that most won't. It wasn't always this easy, though, and I had to push past a comfort zone to do this. I got more comfortable with it by reminding myself that I always meet the coolest people in the most unusual places.

> " *The hardest thing to see is what is in front of your eyes.* "
>
> -Goethe

When You Can't See What's Right In Front of You

Sometimes, though, our self-talk creates blind spots. If you tell yourself something is an obstacle, you're creating a blind spot to the possibilities. When that happens, you can actually be looking right at something and not see it. Beliefs can easily cause us to become blind to the obvious.

Think about this: Have you ever been running frantically around your house looking for your keys, or maybe rummaging in your office looking for a file, the entire time telling yourself you can't find it? Then someone walks in and says, It's right here! Your keys could have been in your hand the whole time, but because of what you were telling yourself, you didn't see them.

The same thing applies at a networking event. If you walk in with the self-talk of "I'm not good at this," "No one ever meets anyone at these things," and so on, you'll miss fantastic connections! This is where curiosity turns the situation around to your benefit. When you're curious, you focus on asking questions and looking for new connections instead of hanging out with people you already know.

An experiment developed by psychologists Daniel Simons and Christopher Chabris shows how our expectations can lead to "inattentional blindness." In their experiment, participants are asked to watch a twenty-five-second video of six people playing basketball. Three people in white shirts are passing a basketball between themselves, and three in black shirts are doing the same. Then, a person in a gorilla suit walks into the middle of the game, beats its chest, and walks off. The gorilla is blatantly obvious to the casual viewer, but when participants are asked to count how many times the basketball is tossed between the people wearing white shirts, they don't see the gorilla at all. Having them focus their attention on something else causes complete blindness to something as obvious as a gorilla.

We also experience blind spots when we focus on the wrong things. If we focus on what's not going right (back to those alligators again), and what's not happening the way that it should be, we don't see all the things that are going right. If you want to "see" a blind spot, try reframing your perspective. An easy way to do this is to ask questions. When we start asking questions, it gets us out of those areas where we were stuck.

Keep asking questions. Ask them in your business, ask for feedback from your team, ask for insights outside of your industry, just keep asking. Find out what else is out there.

If you don't know what questions to ask, you can start with simple ones like, What would it look like, why does it matter, and how can I do this differently? If whatever questions you start with aren't giving you the results that you want, then you need to shift the questions. When you're stuck in a situation, take the typical questions off the table, along with the typical answers, and then ask, "If I can't do that, what else can I do? What else is out there? What else am I looking for?"

Asking questions will open you up to new opportunities, and really change the focus of how you're looking at the problem before you. Asking questions helps you see new things that you may not have seen before because of the stories you were telling yourself. This ties back into the beliefs that you may have as an individual or that your company may have that impact the culture and the results that you're getting.

> ❝ The best moments in our lives are not the passive, receptive, relaxing times . . . The best moments usually occur if a person's body or mind is stretched to its limits in a voluntary effort to accomplish something difficult and worthwhile. ❞

-Mihaly Csikszentmihalyi

Finding Your Flow State (Pay attention Eliana!)

Flow is the state where you truly feel in command of what you do. You're performing at your best and it feels effortless. Obstacles don't exist, and that negative self-talk is replaced with positive thoughts. When you're in the zone (as some people call flow), you feel great and time flies.

The concept of flow was discovered by researchers at the University of Chicago, who asked a wide variety of people, "Tell us about a time when you outdid yourself, when you performed at your peak potential." They asked surgeons, ballerinas, chess champs, and others, and they all described what came to be known as a flow state.

The goal is to consistently be able to get in the flow. Being able to work to your peak potential, and tying your work to your "why," gives you energy, and the inner drive and motivation, that will help keep you jazzed and in the flow.

Mihaly Csikszentmihalyi identifies a number of different elements involved in achieving flow:

- There are clear goals every step of the way.
- There is immediate feedback to one's actions.
- There is a balance between challenges and skills.
- Action and awareness are merged.
- Distractions are excluded from consciousness.
- There is no worry of failure.
- Self-consciousness disappears.
- Sense of time becomes distorted.
- The activity becomes an end in itself.

LEAP EXERCISE

Consider trying one or all of these three different pathways to get in your flow state:

1. Match tasks to your skill set. The more a challenge requires you to use your best skills, the more likely you will become absorbed in flow. If you are under-challenged, or find a task too easy, your performance actually suffers and you end up bored or disengaged.

Reflect: What tasks do you find challenging? (In a good way, of course.)

2. Do work you love. By aligning what you're best at doing with what engages you (what you love to do) and what fits with your "why," you'll enter a frame of mind where flow can arise spontaneously.

Reflect: Think back to the last time you were fully engaged with work to the point that the day flew by, you were super productive, and you felt in the zone. How can you spend more time doing work you love?

3. Get fully focused. The more deeply you can concentrate on a task, the more likely you are to drop into flow while you're doing it. The other paths to flow depend on getting the externals right—the challenge/demand ratio, or finding work that aligns with excellence and engagement. Full focus is an inner dimension. The better your ability to pay attention to what you choose and ignore distractions, the stronger your concentration.

Reflect: Simple breathing exercises can help you to be more centered and focused. If you would like to take it up a notch, try meditation or even yoga.

How do you spend your day? How much time do you spend fixing versus creating and building? Obstacles need to be overcome and problems need to be solved. Opportunities just sit there, waiting for you. Remind yourself often to stay curious, keep looking for the gorilla, and find your flow state.

> *You must have a mindset to always look for and create new opportunities. If a door closes, look for another door that opens.*
>
> -Jerry Bruckner

Milton Berle said, "If opportunity doesn't knock, build a door." I'll add to that: if building a door takes too long, then blast through the wall with a little dynamite.

The opportunities are there. Just look up. You've got to look up.

FIVE

Tigger and George S. Patton:
It's about How High You Bounce

❝I don't measure a man's success on how high he climbs but on how high he bounces when he hits the bottom.❞

-General George S. Patton

We all have experienced, and will continue to have, challenging times, both in business and in our personal lives. In order to be successful, we have to be resilient and be able to bounce back from challenges. It doesn't really matter what the challenge is; it's how you respond to the challenge that makes the biggest difference in bouncing back. Taking leaps means facing new challenges. In order to successfully face new challenges, you'll need to build resilience. Challenges help us appreciate what's on the other side. You may be familiar with the phrase, "without light, there wouldn't be dark; without dark, there wouldn't be light." When you experience both ends of the spectrum, things make more sense, and you're able to truly appreciate where you're at and where you want to go.

You're going to have lessons and then you're going to have lessons. Some are small and some are major, and some will teach you how to bounce back. Resilience means you learn from the setbacks rather than getting hung up on them. Even if something happens in your personal life, you can apply the lesson in your business life, and vice versa.

❝What lies behind us and what lies before us are tiny matters compared to what lies within us.❞

-Ralph Waldo Emerson

You're Stronger Than You Think

Losing both of my parents within a couple years was a huge lesson in resilience. My dad was 81 years old and had been struggling with Parkinson's; after getting an infection and going to the hospital, he quickly deteriorated.

Then, about a year after my dad passed, my mom started showing signs of dementia. I became the on-call person for my mom because I had the most flexible schedule and lived close to the nursing home.

Back then I was a control freak; I always had everything planned out and I didn't like anything getting in the way of my schedule. My schedule was my comfort zone, and having it change in an instant was very unsettling. At first, I associated a change of schedule with something bad, because it meant my mom had fallen or there was another problem. But over time, I came to look at schedule changes as an opportunity for something else—something good—to happen.

Losing my father was so incredibly hard, and then I lost my mom, all before my forty-fifth birthday. Through it all, I just had to keep looking up. It sometimes feels like you're going to die when you're on that kind of emotional roller coaster, but you won't; that's when you find that inner strength and that resilience to keep going, and you discover that the challenging times make you stronger. You learn how to bounce back and get to an even better place than you were before.

A key piece of this is trusting that you can handle whatever comes your way. On my way to speak at a women's conference, I had a great conversation with the marine sitting next to me on the plane, Gary, who had served three tours. I told him that at the conference I would be speaking about the three keys to staying sane in a slightly crazy world, which is really about resilience. I shared with him a great quote from Mother Teresa that I always use in these talks: "God doesn't give you anything you can't handle; I just wish he didn't trust me so much." Gary told me that the marines have a different version of the quote: "God doesn't give you anything you can't handle. I just wish he didn't think I was such a bad ass."

It's true; we often seem to be given more than we can handle, but we just have to remember that we can get through it.

And again, it's how we respond to what happens that makes the biggest difference.

Helen Keller is a great example. She is a symbol of courage, strength, and determination in the face of overwhelming odds. As a child she fell ill and lost her sight and her hearing and fell mute. Technology was far from advanced in her day, and she could easily have chosen to succumb to the yes buts, what ifs, and I don't know how tos. But with the help of her teacher, Anne Sullivan, and other supporters, she turned her challenges into opportunities which helped her find her vision and her voice. The impact she made on others' lives is extraordinary. She wrote: "For, after all, every one who wishes to gain true knowledge must climb the Hill of Difficulty alone, and since there is no royal road to the summit, I must zigzag it in my own way. I slip back many times, I fall, I stand still, I run against the edge of hidden obstacles, I lose my temper and find it again and keep it better, I trudge on, I gain a little, I feel encouraged, I get more eager and climb higher and begin to see the widening horizon. Every struggle is a victory. One more effort and I reach the luminous cloud, the blue depths of the sky, the uplands of my desire."

Life is either a daring adventure or nothing. To keep our faces toward change and behave like free spirits in the presence of fate is strength undefeatable.

-Helen Keller

Power Tools

There are tools that can help you cultivate resilience, such as affirmations. The affirmation that I used during all of the challenging times with my parents was, "I am strong and resilient." There were times I would say that a hundred times a day.

Now, my conscious brain, which is in control about 5 percent of the time, was going, "Yeah, right, you're not doing well. Truly, you are lying." But on the subconscious side, I just kept thinking, "Okay, something is going to stick, something is going to stick." The affirmations were a reminder to keep looking up and keep looking at the light at the end of the tunnel. (You can read more about creating and using affirmations in Chapter 7.)

In addition to using affirmations, I also like to have a theme song. Right now I like "Happy" by Pharrell Williams. You need to find one that works for you, something that, when you're having one of those days, it can get you out of it a little bit. Listening to a song that empowers you or makes you happy gives your body and your mind just a little bit of a break so you can calm down for a minute and refocus. It's also a great kick start to your morning, with or without coffee!

During those tough times, I also had to practice deep breathing and have that circle around me, those friends whom I could reach out to when I needed emotional support. It's okay to ask for help when you need it! I used to think I could handle it all and didn't want to bother anyone, so I kept everything to myself, but that was the wrong thing to do. Remember, if you don't take care of you, no one else will, and sometimes you simply can't do it alone.

> **The best gift anyone could ever give themselves is letting go of people or things who make them feel like crap in order to fully experience what's yet to come.**
>
> -Isaiah Harden

Unfortunately, in addition to those who do truly support you, you may also have some people in your life who don't really want you to bounce back, or they don't want you to move forward or meet your true potential. When you take leaps, you'll push other people's comfort zones as well as your own. They may not realize it's happening, but the emotional effect on them is the same as if they were taking the leap themselves. When this happens, they may unintentionally do things to sabotage your efforts so they can feel more comfortable.

I hate to say it, but if this is happening, you may have to let go of them. That's more difficult with family and other people we can't help but be connected to, but you can limit the amount of time you spend together or set boundaries so you share less with them. They may not always realize that they are raining on your parade, so to speak; they may be doing it because they don't want to see you get hurt. But you need to lead your own life, and you need to be careful whom you allow to support you in that process.

Sometimes, you start to compare your experiences to what other people have gone through; perhaps their experience was worse, or not as bad as, what you're going through, but it doesn't matter—your journey is your journey. All that matters is what you're going through, what's going on with you, and how you can move through that.

And once the storm is over, you won't remember how you made it through, how you managed to survive. You won't even be sure whether the storm is really over. But one thing is certain. When you come out of the storm, you won't be the same person who walked in. That's what this storm's all about.

-Haruki Murakami

A Shift in Perspective

Unfortunately, some of the best lessons are the most difficult. When I lost my horse of 21 years in a fire, I was devastated. I suffered from post-traumatic stress from seeing the barn burn, and literally shook for days after because of the trauma.

The fire happened on Christmas night, and I had a keynote I was delivering on January 3, so there wasn't a lot of time for me to get my act together, but I knew that I had to, no matter what I was experiencing, in order to keep my commitment to my client. And because I work for myself, it was all on me; there was nobody else to rely on to help.

I had to look up, pull it together, and know I could do it. I put my game face on, and I went in and delivered. It was still a lot to process, of course, and sometimes I had to break down when I was away from everybody else.

The experience with my horse, and with my parents, gave me a lot of perspective. Now I realize that no matter how big the obstacles I'm facing, it's not life or death. I may not know how to deal with the challenges, but nobody's going to die.

Of course it's different for a fireman, or a police officer, or a doctor, but for most of us, nobody dies, and we can always figure it out. And if we can't, we surround ourselves with the people who can, and we figure it out together.

> **"I've missed more than 9,000 shots in my career. I've lost almost 300 games. 26 times, I've been trusted to take the game-winning shot and missed. I've failed over and over again in my life. And that is why I succeed."**
>
> -Michael Jordan

A Shark Tale

Barbara Corcoran from *Shark Tank*, the show about pitching business ideas to successful entrepreneurs, has a great story about bouncing back in business. When she was just starting out in real estate, she got this great idea to put her properties on videotape. She spent $77,000 to record every one of the properties, and they called it "Homes on Tape."
It failed big time.

At that point in her business she didn't have that money to lose, so she was in a tough spot. But then Barbara's husband told her about this new thing called the Internet, and she decided to put "Homes on Tape" out on the Internet. Within two weeks, they had sold two properties to individuals in Europe. She'd taken a $77,000 mistake and turned it into a huge success.

The lesson here is that when something happens, we need to acknowledge the fact that we made a mistake, but then we have to focus past that to where we're going. Keep going up that staircase that we talked about in the beginning of the book, a step at a time. Determination to keep going no matter what's happening around you is a big part of being resilient.

Your mind can be your greatest ally or your greatest adversary. You have to recognize what your thoughts are, pause for a minute, and put everything into perspective.

We often think that we'll never recover from a tragedy. But just because you're going through something difficult doesn't mean you won't be able to bounce back and inspire others.

You will have tough days, and it's okay to have a minor meltdown now and then. But then you have to pause and ask yourself, "What do I need to do to get out of it? Can I do it on my own? Do I need to call a friend or family member? Do I need to get a theme song playing on iTunes, or should I choose an affirmation and write it on my mirror?"

Figure out what will help you get through, and don't forget to look up! You've got to look up long enough to know that there's truly light at the end of the tunnel.

> ❝ *Life doesn't get easier or more forgiving; we get stronger and more resilient.* ❞
>
> -Steve Maraboli

Building Resilience

Resilience is vitally important to the success of an organization. It's a fact of life that s*** happens—and usually when you least expect it. When a team is resilient, they will collaborate to solve problems. Be sure to publicly applaud them for their response.

Making mistakes is an important part of resilience because it builds strength. If a person has never been allowed to fail, he or she may implode at the smallest challenge. Adopt a "'fess it and fix it" attitude within your organization.

Communication is also key. Resilient cultures encourage people to ask questions during difficult times. It's easier to tackle challenges when the talk around the water cooler is focused on what we can do, versus telling them not to worry about it (because they will anyway).

Resilient companies are agile, adaptable, and willing to pivot if needed. Companies who put the proverbial blinders on end up in a reactive state instead of a proactive state. It takes more time, resources, and revenue to put out fires that were never considered. Focus on success but plan for failure, and don't be surprised when it happens. Put a strategy in place, including a team that can calmly address the situation, and avoid blaming at all costs.

Resilience ultimately is about mindset—that of the leadership and of the other people in the organization.

Successful people view failure as an opportunity for personal growth, and they use their failures to gain knowledge and experience.

Remember, the only time you fail is when you refuse to get back up. You're never a failure until you quit.

Resilient people:
- Have a fire in their belly that compels them to get out of bed in the morning (their "why")
- Focus their time and energy on changing the things they have control over
- See the effects of bad events as temporary, not permanent
- Set goals and have the courage to go after their dreams, even with the risk that they might fail
- Choose how they respond
- Have a positive image of the future (they know there's a pony in the pile of manure)

Too often we let our mistakes and setbacks define who we are. Dr. Martin Seligman, the founder of Positive Psychology, once said, "It's not our failures that determine our future success, but how we explain them to ourselves." If you knew that no matter what happened, you could handle it, what actions would you take that you aren't taking now? What conversations would you have that you've been putting off? Where would you step out onto center stage more fully and boldly in your own life—and in doing so, open up the possibility for new opportunities, new relationships, new ideas to take bloom?

LEAP EXERCISE

Challenges and Accomplishments
1. Write 10 challenges that you've faced or are facing.
2. When done, put S, G, or SG next to each one, depending on if each was more closely related to survival, growth, or both.
3. Reflect on the biggest lesson you learned from each challenge.
4. Write down how each lesson made you stronger and more resilient.
5. Post this list where you can see it regularly, and keep adding to it!

Resilience may be an art, the ultimate art of living . . . At the heart of resilience is a belief in oneself—yet also a belief in something larger than oneself. Resilient people do not let adversity define them. They find resilience by moving towards a goal beyond themselves, transcending pain and grief by perceiving bad times as a temporary state of affairs.

-Hara Estroff Marano

SIX
Grow Your Wings on the Way Down

❝ *Only those who dare to fail greatly can ever achieve greatly.* **❞**

-Robert F. Kennedy

The idea of the comfort zone goes back to a famous experiment conducted by psychologists Robert M. Yerkes and John D. Dodson way back in 1908. Using mice, they found that stimulation improved performance, but only up to a certain level—if there is too much stimulation, performance starts to decrease. "Optimal anxiety" is the level at which we perform our best, and it's just outside our comfort zone. When we start to feel too anxious, however, our subconscious will attempt to pull us back to our "normal." But when you begin to get comfortable with being a little uncomfortable, you will be able to take bigger leaps with less anxiety.

❝ *A year from now you will wish you had started today.* **❞**

-Karen Lamb

Pulling a MacGyver

Taking a leap can be one of the scariest things you've ever done, but it's worth it. Remember, you don't have to have all the answers before you leap. One of my favorite quotes to illustrate this idea comes from David Brinkley: "She took a leap of faith and grew her wings on the way down." Some might say it's like building your plane while you're flying it, or just figuring it out as you go, but the point is the same: When you jump without all the answers, you learn to think on your feet, and that's where innovation comes from, where creativity blossoms, and where even greater success is possible.

Some people jump on their own, but others get thrown into a situation they weren't ready for and are still able to make it work. For example, I met a man at a conference where I was speaking who had to take over his family's business when he was just 18 years old, because his father had a heart attack.

Some people would run from a situation like this, but he dove in, and ended up doing very well.

I used to be the kind of person who would back down from challenges. My self-talk told me that I couldn't handle change; it was too scary. I didn't have the necessary knowledge and wasn't sure where I would find the resources. That mindset came from my experiences in personal relationships, including a verbally abusive relationship that put me in a shell.

I didn't have the belief that I could really create and do the things that I wanted to do. I was afraid to step outside my comfort zone. I was afraid of making a mistake. But as I changed my beliefs about who I was and what I could do, my perspective on change and challenges shifted as well. Now, I purposefully push myself. If there's a challenge, great! And frankly, as long as you have a supportive community, YouTube, or Google, you can figure out just about anything. At least that's what I've discovered.

For example, when my car needed coolant, I wanted to take care of it myself but wasn't sure how, so I searched on YouTube, and within three minutes I found a video that showed me how to check the coolant level. Resources are all around you if you're open to looking.

I learned to think on my feet doing Table Topics in Toastmasters. For this exercise, either they volunteer you or you volunteer yourself. You get up in the front of the room and they give you a topic and say, "Start." You have 60 seconds to say whatever you're going to say about that particular topic. Talk about figuring it out as you go!

When you're willing to put yourself in a situation that feels uncomfortable, it's like pulling a MacGyver. Do you remember that show? The main character, secret agent Angus MacGyver, was always able to find a way out of tricky situations. He often figured it out with just seconds to spare, but there was always a way.

A great habit to get into is to spend 5–10 minutes at the end of each day to mentally run through the following day's events. Think about the meetings you have planned: who they are with, the agenda, and what outcomes you're looking for. What else is on your to-do list? When you take the time to plan in advance, you can hit the ground running the next day. Remember, things don't always go as planned, so consider what you will do if you encounter a potential pivot moment where you need to decide whether to change course.

Remember, everything that you are familiar with today was once unfamiliar territory.

There was a time when you didn't know how to walk, talk, or read, but you probably do all of those things effortlessly now. Keep trying until you succeed, and you'll be amazed at how quickly you progress.

> *Be brave. Take risks.*
> *Nothing can substitute experience.*

-Paulo Coelho

Mindfulness and Trust

Growing wings on the way down takes courage, so it's important to trust your decisions. You often know the answer in your gut; you know what you have to do, but it still feels uncomfortable to do it. But it's hard to listen to yourself when you have a never-ending to-do list, an inbox full of emails that multiply like rabbits, and a day filled with back-to-back meetings.

To uncover the answer in your gut, you may have to make a concerted effort to get quiet for a little bit. It may help to practice mindfulness, a state of consciousness that allows you to be open to new things through having an uncluttered mind. Companies like Google and Intel have adopted programs that teach employees how to use mindfulness techniques to find clarity and solutions to the challenges they encounter. It's been shown that the practice can raise effectiveness and create space for creative thinking. Practicing mindfulness allows you to get centered and focused to be able to listen to your gut.

> *The most valuable thing you can make is a mistake—*
> *you can't learn anything from being perfect.*

-Adam Osborne

Fail Forward

Failure can be tough to swallow, but we should actually be grateful for all of our failures, because we can learn from them. Not everyone may agree with this, but I'm a firm believer that when something fails, it's because things weren't supposed to work out the way we thought they should. As my oldest brother, Steve, says, "Everything happens for a reason, and it happens exactly as it's supposed to."

It might not be obvious in the moment, but sometimes the most challenging experiences turn out to be blessings in disguise. Steve Jobs once said, "I didn't see it then, but it turned out that getting fired from Apple was the best thing that could have ever happened to me. The heaviness of being successful was replaced by the lightness of being a beginner again, less sure about everything. It freed me to enter one of the most creative periods of my life." Jobs certainly experienced disappointment and failure, but taking risks also helped him experience incredible success.

Richard Branson is another example of someone who has been successful despite the challenges and failures he had along the way. He's dyslexic, and he dropped out of school. Then he started building companies and had some massive failures, but now, his Virgin Group holds about 400 companies around the world. Branson had his vision; he had a solid plan, he was willing to take big risks, and he had to readjust in the process, constantly changing, in order to have the success that he sees today.

Learn from your failures:

Ask what you can do better.
Decide to learn from everyone.
Demand brutal analysis of your actions.
Stop whining.
Fear less.
Let yourself be inspired.
Have a plan.
Choose to be invincible.
Ask more questions.
Plan to be successful.
Be an expert.
Decide to take action today.
Seek and find answers to your questions.

Fight mediocrity.
Be accountable.
Work on your biggest weakness.
Create what's missing.
Practice getting back up.
Intentionally put yourself in tough places.
Try something new.
Have a purpose each day.
Don't stop until you finish.
Imagine the possibilities.
Fail gracefully.

As I've said, I used to be very much of a control freak. It had to go my way; it had to be this way; it had to be in this amount of time. But when my mom was struggling with dementia, there were days that I had to drop everything or reschedule everything on last minute's notice. Eventually, I got to the point that I was okay with it. It was a big mindset shift for me, but I knew I was learning from the experience and I learned to let go. And, sometimes, by not pushing and forcing, something better happened. (It also significantly reduced my stress levels.)

It's essential to set goals, both short-term and long-term. For example, you can look at five-year goals, three-year goals, and one-year goals. But you also have to remember that a missile doesn't always get to its target in a straight line. This is especially true in business, because of how fast things are changing in the world. Sometimes, that target is going to move, but as long as you're flexible, you can find the best way to get there by thinking outside the box. Remember, when things don't go smoothly, do the post-mortem that we talked about earlier.

Pivot if needed, keep moving and fail forward.

Really cool opportunities and synergies in business can happen when you're open to possibilities, because you're looking at things differently. And, sometimes, when you're looking for answers, you're going to get even greater solutions than you ever dreamed.

When you fail it puts you in a place where you're more desperate and more motivated. You're always better when you're hungry than when you're sated. Also, success is false protection because the heat gets taken off you. For me, fear and confusion are sometimes good places to start.

-Willem Dafoe, actor

Building the Plane While Flying It

To realize the impossible requires taking the right risks and not being afraid of change. This next story is a great example of that. Walt Disney was a forward thinker who embraced change, and his company, now 90 years old, still embodies that philosophy. A number of years ago, Anne Sweeney, the head of Disney/ABC Television, was traveling a lot and wanted to take her shows with her everywhere. She understood the audience perspective, not just the executive's perspective, and it changed her mission at work. She moved Disney into the digital age by allowing the iTunes store to sell TV shows viewable on the iPod. (This was in 2005, before the iPad and iPhone.) A year later, they made it possible for viewers to watch shows through ABC.com. Later, Anne led the leap to launch WATCH ABC, an app that live-streams TV shows and video on demand. The first response from her team wasn't a positive one—the technology was still in development and there were a lot of obstacles to overcome—but she eventually convinced them to not only take on the project but move up the launch date by an entire year. Meeting the launch deadline was a very close call, but they made it happen. Anne says that she's surrounded by change every day. As a result, she says, "I don't have a lot of fear, for good and bad. We have a culture at Disney that is very, very fast paced and forward thinking."

It's kind of fun to do the impossible.

-Walt Disney

Flying Through Turbulence

Sometimes it's not about taking big risks and building the plane while you're flying it, but keeping it flying in the face of turbulence.

A few years ago, I worked with a small organization in Kansas that works with individuals with disabilities. Because of all the Medicare laws that were changing in the State of Kansas, they were going through massive upheaval within the organization. They were losing some of their funding, and they were going to have to restructure their 70-person business.

On top of everything else, some members of the leadership team were struggling with challenges in their personal lives.

I did a workshop for the entire organization, and then I spent two full days with the leadership team. On the first day, when I walked in the room, they looked like they'd been beaten up. The CEO had told me that, every day, they were having meetings first thing in the morning to put out fires. That's how rapidly things were changing. Things were being mandated at the state level, and they had no control over what was happening.

This organization had been recognized at the state level, as well as the national level, for their model and their accomplishments, but with everything they were going through, they'd lost the fire in their belly.

The more we got into the process of shifting their mindset so they could develop a new strategic plan, the more the energy in the room shifted. And at the end of the first day, I asked them, "Would you rather come to work with the energy that you had when you first got in this room? Or would you rather experience the energy you're feeling now? It's not that the problems are all going to go away tomorrow, but your perspective and how you are working together will change. That group dynamic is going to change, and it will impact everybody within the organization."

At the end of the second day, we had come up with a lot of creative ideas around marketing, how to get the vision out, how to communicate to the individuals they were serving, and how to get to their "why." By getting that "why" back, they could develop the fire, passion, and drive that would improve the culture so they could move forward.

The insights created within that team helped them not just at a company level but also at an individual level, and, sometimes, that's what it boils down to.

Even in business, it's about the individual. And if you can make change in your own life and have the tools to help you get through the darkest times, then imagine how that will impact the organization in return.

> ❝ *Jump, and you will find out how to unfold your wings as you fall.* ❞
>
> -Ray Bradbury

Imagine the Possibilities

When you allow your mind to dream of possibilities, all constraints and preconceptions can disappear. Start by asking yourself questions that begin with phrases such as these:

How might I . . . ?
What's stopping us from . . . ?
In what ways could I . . . ?
What would happen if . . . ?

From there, you can ask follow-up questions, like:

Why would we . . . ?
What has to change to allow us to . . . ?
Who would need to . . . ?
When should I . . . ?

At this stage there's no reason to place limits on your imagination. What's the can't-do that you wish were a can-do? The future problem you could start solving now? The half-baked notion you'd like to see a reality? Where is the place where the suddenly possible meets the desperately necessary? Dreaming allows you to leave the realm of limitations, if only for a few moments, to imagine a future worth pursuing.

Successful people understand that failure is absolutely essential to achievements; without it, there is no growth or experience gained.

The greats became great because they didn't fear the idea of failing. They didn't get there by playing small. They had to be willing to risk it. They had to risk getting uncomfortable. They had to risk taking the leap, going all in with a swan dive.

You can't be concerned about what others are going to think if you do fail. Stick to your idea, your vision. You have a plan. You're willing to be flexible, but you have that passion, that desire, that fire in the belly that will get you where you want to go. When you take that leap of faith, you can grow beyond your wildest dreams.

Seven
You Can't Just Visualize
and Then Go Eat a Sandwich

**" *To accomplish great things we must first dream, then
visualize, then plan . . . believe . . . act!* "**

-Alfred Montapert

Creating a new habit, achieving a new goal, or pushing a comfort zone sounds
good in theory. Having a plan to get there is important, but just as important
are the mental tools that make change easier, such as creative visualization and
affirmations. First, we'll take a closer look at visualization.

Visualization in Practice

I won't profess to be a huge football fan, but I love the commercials, especially
during the Superbowl. One of my favorites was the 2012 Kia commercial[4].
It's nighttime, and you see Mr. Sandman tiptoeing from the closet and across
a couple's bedroom. He makes his way to the woman's side of the bed, and
sprinkles a spoonful of dream dust on her. She smiles, and then you're taken
into the middle of her dream. She is sitting behind an attractive guy on a white
horse, galloping across a beautiful meadow. Then Mr. Sandman tiptoes to the
other side of the bed and accidentally trips over a pair of slippers, causing him
to dump the entire pouch of dream dust on the sleeping guy. Next, you see
and hear the squeal of tires and see Mötley Crüe on stage performing their
heart-pounding '80s hit "Kickstart My Heart." The guy is driving the Kia
Optima around the racetrack at full speed. A supermodel holds the checkered
flag, and the screaming spectators are bikini-clad women. There's a guy riding
a giant bull, two lumberjacks sawing apart a giant sandwich, and an MMA
fight—this is clearly a guy's dream. You see Mr. Sandman in the bedroom,
frantically trying to wipe the dream dust off, and he finally gives up. At the
end of the commercial, the guy drives his car through the racetrack wall and
ends up in the meadow, where he spins out. The horse rears up, the woman
lands in his arms, and they drive off together. Whether you have seen the
commercial or not, you probably got some kind of image in your mind as I

was describing it. What you just experienced was visualization.

> ❝ *I don't believe you have to be better than everybody else. I believe you have to be better than you ever thought you could be.* ❞
>
> -Ken Venturi

Applying Creative Visualization

Your subconscious doesn't think in words; it can only think in pictures. Creative visualization is the technique of using one's imagination to visualize specific behaviors or events occurring in one's life. It is a way to unblock or dissolve barriers that we ourselves have created. You have to believe that what you are thinking about is possible in some way, even though you don't know how to make it happen.

Ideas start in the imagination, and creative visualization helps us see those ideas as reality and increases our motivation. Creative visualization can be used to improve virtually anything, from your golf game to your bottom line. It's not a substitute for taking action, but provides a clear picture of your desired outcomes. It has the ability to strengthen your belief of what is possible before you actually experience the reality.

Visualization is sometimes called mental imagery or mental rehearsal. If you are doing a simple visualization, you picture a setting, another person, or a sequence of events—something outside yourself. Visualization can be both visual and kinesthetic. Kinesthetic is experiential, so when you are visualizing yourself in a setting, and creating in your mind the experience of doing something, you might feel the sensations in your body.

Athletes use this more kinesthetic type of visualization to help improve their performance. Golf legend Jack Nicklaus is said to always play a course in his mind before actually beginning a game. In his own words: "I never hit a shot, not even in practice, without having a very sharp, in-focus picture of it in my head. First I see the ball where I want it to finish, nice and white and sitting up high on the bright-green grass. Then the scene quickly changes, and I see the ball going there: its path, trajectory, and shape, even its behavior on landing. Then there is a sort of fade-out, and the next scene shows me making the kind of swing that will turn the previous images into reality."

Did you notice how detailed he was in describing it, from the colors to the feel of swinging his golf club? Visualization works best when you get really specific and focus on all of the senses.

Another example of effectively using creative visualization comes from Jim Carrey. He wanted to be a movie star, and he wanted to have millions of dollars in his bank account. So he wrote out a huge check to himself, and he was constantly visualizing cashing that check.

Jim stuck with it long enough to make it a reality, but not everyone does. What often happens is that, based on our experience in life, we don't have that true belief in ourselves to make that big of a leap, and to believe it's really possible. Creative visualization won't work because our subconscious still doesn't believe it's possible.

This is especially true if you shoot for something that's too big. For example, you might say, "I want to be worth a hundred million dollars," and you have just a thousand dollars in your bank account. It's too big of a leap. That's not to say it can't happen, but the odds of winning the lottery aren't good enough for you to stake everything on a ticket. You have to do the work, too! At the same time, your subconscious is going to be working against you, because it's thinking, "I can't do that. How am I even doing that?" So you talk yourself out of it and you don't even realize it.

> **❝Peak performers develop powerful mental images of the behavior that will lead to the desired results. They see in their mind's eye the result they want, and the actions leading to it.❞**
>
> -Charles A. Garfield

When you set a goal and continuously visualize the end result, this creates the drive and energy to change reality so that it matches the picture you have been visualizing. Start by thinking about what you want tomorrow to look like. If you have a big meeting tomorrow, you could visualize that meeting being the best meeting ever. You would mentally rehearse it by thinking it through: *If the client says this, how will I respond?* That way, you'll feel more comfortable in the meeting, and more confident that it will go well.

So you want to focus not just on the end goal, but each step along the way. Say, for example, you're planning a party, and you see it in your mind. You may already do this and think of it as "forethought," which is just another word for creative visualization: Who is going to be there? What does the table look like, what type of appetizers are you serving, what type of meal, what's the atmosphere in the room? Do you have music playing?

People tend to spend more time planning vacations and parties than they do using this process to make intentional changes in their life or business. When you visualize and see the details in a more practical sense, you know how to put it all together to make that vision a reality, and you can use that for everything from a vacation to a business process.

When I was first learning to give a speech, I was terrified, so I used visualization to help get myself comfortable with being in front of an audience before I was actually there. I would feel myself going through the motions, hearing the sound of my voice, and seeing how I was interacting, just like an athlete would do for a sports performance.

Visualization actually triggers muscle memory, which is why it can be so effective, as shown in this study conducted by Dr. Blaslotto at the University of Chicago. He split people into three groups and tested each group on how many free throws they could make. Then, he had the first group practice free throws every day for an hour. The second group just visualized themselves making free throws, without actually practicing. The third group did nothing. After 30 days, he tested them again. The first group improved by 24 percent. The second group improved by 23 percent—without touching a basketball!—and the third group did not improve, which was expected.

Visualization is a simple process but, like anything new, it takes time to get comfortable doing it.

The best natural times to use visualization are just before you fall asleep and when you awaken. At these times you are closest to the alpha state of consciousness, which is the day-dreaming state. Sit in a comfortable position. It may help to be in a quiet space so you can focus. Close your eyes. Don't worry if you start to see an image and then your mind comes back to the present moment. You want this to be enjoyable and relaxing. Say you're trying to visualize a beach, but it just isn't working. Instead, you can think of an experience when you were having a great time and laughing. It could be as simple as shopping with a friend or spending time with your family.

Start with a basic outline and then keep adding details. Sometimes it helps to write the visualization out and read it as you imagine the details. The goal is to create a mental image while you're reading. Remember to use all five senses: What do you see, what do you feel, what do you hear, what does it smell like, taste like? There isn't any right or wrong; it's all up to you and what works best.

When you're visualizing, the more that you can put yourself in the midst of the experience you want to have, the more effective it will be. So think about something you really got jazzed about—the last big win you had, the last time you closed a deal, when a check arrived from a client—and tap into that feeling. Think about what that feeling was, and how you can re-create it, as well as thinking about everything that went into having the experience.

> *It's the repetition of affirmations that leads to belief. And once belief becomes a deep conviction, things begin to happen.*
>
> -Claude M. Bristol

The Power of Affirmations

Every thought you think and everything you say is an affirmation. Affirmations are not an end result; they are a means to get you to your end result. They consciously shift your self-talk.

When using affirmations, keep in mind you may feel a tug-of-war between your conscious and subconscious mind. You're consciously stating your desired end result in the present tense, and your subconscious may push back with, "Yes, but that's not how I am now." That's why combining affirmations with visualization makes it easier and more powerful.

To some, affirmations may sound abstract, but they can be practical. Instead of trying to sound really deep or profound, make it a point to write affirmations that speak to your life. They don't need to be exceptionally long or detailed, but they should definitely be specific to you. Think of the future outcome you are seeking and then put it in the present tense.

Affirmations should:

- Be written in first-person present tense: "I am . . . ," "I choose to . . ."
- Use positive active verbs: "I feel confident and my words flow smoothly and easily."
- Be specific: "It feels good to have lost 10 pounds," instead of, "I want to lose weight."
- Be believable: For example, if you're currently making $35,000 a year and you write an affirmation that you're currently making $200,000, it's too much of a stretch.

LEAP EXERCISE

Think of a goal, habit or leap you're working on and write an affirmation for it.

Affirmations are a powerful tool. If you're a visual person, be sure to keep your affirmations front and center (I like to write them on the bathroom mirror). If you find that affirmations aren't working for you, try *afformations*. Noah St. John created the concept of afformations by putting affirmations in the form of a question, which helps your subconscious go to work to find the answer; some people find this approach easier. (You can check out Noah's book *The Great Little Book of Afformations* for more information.)

> ❝ *There are two things people want more than sex and money . . . recognition and praise.* ❞
>
> -Mary Kay Ash

Celebrate Your Wins

When you do have a success, it's important to celebrate. Wins tie back to the visualization because you have a chance to feel the experience. Then you can easily reflect back on what you've accomplished and use it to go after your next goal, your next comfort zone. Celebrating wins helps you maintain motivation.

A lot of us tend to focus on what we didn't get done, what wasn't accomplished, and what's left on the to-do list, which can be discouraging. But if instead we focus on what we did accomplish and our wins for the day, no matter how small, it keeps things positive and we feel motivated to keep going.

An easy way to track personal wins is to keep a journal. Write your big and small successes in your journal and refer back to it often. Another option is to think of three things each day that you're grateful for. These are the good things that have happened to you; it could be as simple as a compliment you gave or received, something that made you laugh, or a new business connection. This is especially helpful when creating new habits and goals and pushing comfort zones, because it builds confidence and self-esteem.

I do this for myself, and with the teams I work with. Strategizing on ways to track wins is an important part of the process because appreciation and recognition are essential in creating a culture of excellence. People want to be respected and valued for their contribution to the team. We all have the need to be recognized as an individual or member of a group and to feel a sense of achievement for work well done. It is important to stay aware of the impact that timely recognition of achievement can have on the team, and on the bottom line. Be sure each person is recognized in some way, no matter how small their accomplishments. Otherwise, their self-talk could sabotage their performance as they start to believe that they never get any wins.

LEAP EXERCISE ▰▰▰▰▰▰▰▰▰▰▰▰▰▰▰▰▰▰▰▰▰▰▰▰▰

Tracking wins in business and your personal life:
- **How do you currently track wins?**
- **What are some new ways you could track wins?**

It's great to put the win list up on a wall, or in a central location, where it will keep everyone motivated and focused on the goal or vision. Celebrate your wins and those of others, no matter how big or how small.

❝ What you get by achieving your goals is not as important as what you become by achieving your goals. ❞

-Henry David Thoreau

Your Mindset Toolbox

So to wrap up, let's put all of the mental tools together.
1. Read your affirmations and visualize the images these words trigger.
2. Create a vivid picture. It should be experiential, where you see yourself

at the level of action, skill, behavior, or emotion that you're affirming into your new normal.

3. Feel the emotion in your accomplishment as if the event is happening right now. It's easier as you get more wins.
4. Recognize accomplishments and track wins!

Now, keep in mind that when you're looking at mindset tools, not everything works for everybody the same way. Figure out what you can easily connect with first, and explore what works best for you. Sometimes, when you force it, it doesn't work, and you get discouraged. You don't have to do them all at once, but it can be a powerful combination when you do them together, because it helps you to clearly see the desired end result as successfully completed. Each time you use this process, you're intentionally shifting your thoughts. Your thoughts accumulate to become beliefs, and your beliefs are powerful!

❝Do not wait: the time will never be 'just right'. Start where you stand, and work whatever tools you may have at your command and better tools will be found as you go along.❞

- **Napoleon Hill**

Eight
Who's Your Kevin Bacon

And that is how change happens. One gesture. One person. One moment at a time.

-Libba Bray

The most powerful insights often come from the most unexpected places—the collective genius of your circle of influence, and other smart people who would be eager to teach you what they know if you simply asked for their insights. This is why it's so important to expand your circle and continually connect with others.

You may have heard of the concept of six degrees of separation, which suggests that everyone and everything is no more than six steps away, by way of introduction, from any other person or thing in the world. Later, some students at Albright College in Pennsylvania created a game out of the concept with the actor Kevin Bacon; the goal is to link any actor to Kevin Bacon through no more than six connections, where two actors are connected if they have appeared in a movie or commercial together. Now, you can even search Google to find out any given actor's Bacon number.

Kevin Bacon was probably chosen for this game because he's been in a lot of movies with a lot of different people, so it's easy to connect him with others. I bet there's someone you know personally who's a lot like Kevin Bacon; he or she seems to be connected to everyone. So why does this matter? In a word: relationships. If you can nurture and maintain relationships with the right people who can help you reach your personal, career, and business goals, you will thrive.

The good news is that you are truly six degrees (or less) of separation away from anyone you want to meet. You just need the right mindset in order to connect with them.

{{ Position yourself as a center of influence, the one who knows the movers and shakers. People will respond to that, and you'll soon become what you project. }}

-Bob Burg

Wallflower to Connector

As I mentioned earlier, for part of my life I was a real wallflower, but eventually I recognized that in order to reach my business and personal goals, that needed to change. The first thing I had to do was get outside my comfort zone with networking, because I was not comfortable in that environment. Watching others go from wallflower to connector gave me the confidence to know that I could do it too. But it got even easier when I learned how creating those connections with people truly starts in your mind. This is because of a mental filter we have called the Reticular Activating System (RAS).

The RAS acts like a filter on your subconscious mind; it sorts out what is important information that needs to be paid attention to and what is unimportant and can be ignored.

There are so many distractions and demands in our everyday life that it seems almost impossible to stay focused at times. Our RAS helps make paying attention and being focused a little bit easier. As I've said before, you're drawn toward what you think about, and that's partly because doing so activates your RAS to seek answers.

Using my RAS has helped me reach my goals, increase my client base, and create my circle of influence. Remember, because the RAS helps you tune in to the information you need, you need to be as specific as possible.

Unfortunately, many people struggle to get specific. Too often, I'm at a networking event and ask someone whom they want to meet. They respond with a vague description of a company, such as "a mid-sized company that wants to grow their bottom line." Or they say they work with everyone or their product is for everyone, or they use so much industry lingo to describe the services they provide that it feels like they're describing a blue elephant.

They can't give me a clear picture of whom they work with or what they do, so I can't possibly connect them. (And it will be difficult for them to make connections on their own, too.)

Your RAS (and I, as a connector) can help you out much more easily when you know that the perfect client for you is an insurance broker with 2–15 salespeople/producers. The owner or CEO of the company may be frustrated with a lack of results from the sales team, or be unsure where to start making changes. They may wish to implement a training program, but do not know where to turn to have the resources necessary to compete in their market.

> *"If you don't go after what you want, you'll never have it. If you don't ask, the answer is always no. If you don't step forward, you're always in the same place."*
>
> -Nora Roberts

Ask!

When you ask for help, and if you do so genuinely, the worst anyone will say is no. Then you are no worse off than if you hadn't asked for help at all! For some this is a comfort zone push, but the effort can be well worth it. In short, get over your yes buts and just make the ask.

For a time I sat on a non-profit board whose focus was working with at-risk girls in the Kansas City, Kansas, School District.

I was gaining more confidence in my networking skills, and having to raise funds for the non-profit pushed me farther outside my comfort zone.

I jokingly say that if you're in fundraising, it means you're going to be kissing a lot of frogs. That's what it takes to get to the princes, the right donors.

One evening I was out with a friend at happy hour. The guy next to us at the bar looked like Bono from U2. We smiled but never spoke. When he went into the restaurant, my curiosity got the best of me, so I asked the waitress who he was. She told me his name was Mark and he was in the petroleum business. Immediately, that *Ding, ding, ding, money!* alarm went off in my head. (As a fundraising chair, you're always listening for those money signs.)

It was my RAS at work!

About a month later, I was having a business breakfast at another restaurant, and Mark was there. I could see that he was looking at me with that look of, *I think I know you but I'm not quite sure from where.* Once again, we didn't talk. About a month later, I was having happy hour again with some old co-workers, and Mark was there. He walked up to me and said, "I think I've met you." I said, "No, but we've seen each other before at happy hour and breakfast."

Mark was there with a gentleman who was a cousin of a restaurateur whom I wanted to meet. I knew the restaurateur could be a great resource for our organization, so I asked Mark if he would introduce me to his friend, and he asked me why. I told him that I was the fundraising chair for a local non-profit, working with at-risk girls in the Kansas City, Kansas, School District, and that I was always looking for people who wanted to donate to our organization and who would be great resources.

Mark said, "Well, I'll give you money." And I said, "Great! I'll take $10,000."

He had a stunned look on his face and I wasn't sure that he heard me so, of course, I repeated, "Really, I'll take $10,000."

He got quiet and I said, "Mark, give me your card. I'll call you Monday," which I did. I found out that, yes, he donated to a number of organizations, including youth charities. So I sent him information, and when we met a week later, he wrote me a check on the spot for $3,500.

Then he said, "There's this guy that you need to meet. His name is Brad. He and his buddies have started a foundation that holds charity golf tournaments and donates the proceeds to other local charities in Kansas City."

When I called Brad, he said, "What great timing you have! We're just now in our selection process."

So I sent him information and connected him to our executive director. That year, Brad's organization picked our charity and another local charity as the beneficiaries of their golf tournament, and we got a check for $15,000.

That whole experience showed me the power of asking. You never know who's in your circle of influence who can lead you to the next person. Even if the person you're asking can't help, there is always one more question to ask (possibly the most important): "Do you know anyone who may be able to help with this?" You would be amazed at how many doors this simple question will open up. Depending on your network, you could be just two degrees from the person you need to meet.

LEAP EXERCISE

Your Ask Challenge

Make an ask that is genuine but makes you feel uncomfortable. Don't hesitate; go do it right now. Ideally, choose something you have wanted to ask of someone for quite some time but have held yourself back. Whether this means asking someone you admire in business to go to lunch, asking an investor if they'd like to invest in your company, or asking a new Facebook friend out for coffee, just make the ask in a sincere and genuine way.

❝You're the average of the five people you spend the most time with.❞

-Jim Rohn

Creating Your Circle of Influence

Your "circle of influence" is everyone you know—your network—especially those key relationships that serve you personally and professionally. This includes family and friends, and other relationships such as your tribe and the strategic referral partners you work with to help build and promote each other's businesses.

I used to be very unintentional in my attempts to connect with people, but I didn't realize it. I attended so many different networking groups in an effort to meet people, but because I wasn't being intentional about it, the majority of the people I was meeting were there to sell me something. It had nothing to do with creating synergistic relationships.

So how do you be more intentional in creating your circle of influence? First, create a relationship plan by asking yourself these questions:

- What are you looking for?
- What do you need the most help with?
- If you could meet anyone, who would it be?
- Who would make great strategic partners in business?

Start by determining who it is that you want to connect with, and, as highlighted by my story about the golf tournament, don't be afraid to ask. There may be a CEO that you want to reach out to or somebody else who's powerful within your network, or right outside your network.

If you have wallflower tendencies, then start by seeing whom you know who knows the person you want to meet; that person can make a warm introduction for you. LinkedIn is a terrific resource for this. If you don't have a mutual connection, then start by sending a handwritten note, and follow up with an email. Ask to take them to lunch or buy them a cup of coffee, and see what information they might be able to share with you. Most importantly, ask how you might be able to help them.

Be genuine when you meet people. What if you treated every person you met with the same enthusiasm you would show when meeting one of your heroes? Imagine how those people would feel. You would not only make a great first impression, but also a lasting impression.

> *It takes 20 years to build a reputation and five minutes to ruin it. If you think about that, you'll do things differently.*
>
> -Warren Buffett

Grow Your Circle Deliberately

To get to where you want to go in life faster, it's all about your support network. It always helps to have somebody who can talk you into your success when you don't see it; it gives you that little boost of confidence to keep going. What I found was that when I had people nudging me and saying, "You're doing a great job; keep this up," and I could also see them leading by example, it gave me that bravery to get out there myself.

You want to focus on filling your circle of influence with people who will support you on your journey from there to here.

Looking at the people within your circle(s) of influence, and those you might choose to add, ask yourself:

- Do the people you associate with encourage you to dream big?
- Do they encourage you to take leaps?
- Do they support your quest for pursuing your passion?
- Are the people in your life positive and upbeat?
- Do they have a reciprocity mindset?
- Do they provide insight and inspiration that challenges you to be a better version of yourself?
- Do their beliefs and values reflect the beliefs and values you'd like to have?
- Do you have fun when you are with them?
- Do you give as much to them as they give to you?

If you don't answer yes to the majority of these questions, then there may be people in your circle of influence who need to go, or who should not be welcomed in. Cultivate relationships with the people you want to be like. Use the power of relationships to boost you towards the next level in your life.

Keep a list of 8–10 big influencers you have a relationship with or want to develop a relationship with. Every 60 days or so, take out the list and evaluate your current relationship with each person on a scale of 1 to 10. If it is less than an 8, develop an action plan on how it can be improved before your next review.

> *If you want to go somewhere, it is best to find someone who has already been there.*
>
> -Robert Kiyosaki

Connecting with Mentors

Good mentors know what it takes to succeed. They aren't your friends or parents. Their role is to tell you what you really need to hear about your business, as well as your personal life. They've been there and done that and can keep you from falling into the same traps. They are inspiring and make great cheerleaders. They are willing to make connections that would be beneficial because someone once helped them and they want to pay it forward.

If you need a mentor or coach for business, look for somebody who is strong in your weak areas, and who has relevant expertise; start by looking for people in your circle of influence who might be able to help you connect with them; they can more easily open doors than you could on your own.

Chemistry is important! You want to make sure it's a good fit, so do your research (social media is a great tool for this); ask several people for their personal experience with this person before you contact them directly. When you connect with someone, you want to be able to tell them concisely the help you need—maybe you need a mentor, or perhaps a coach would be better. A mentor does not charge you for his or her time and will offer you advice and guidance to move forward, typically in a particular business niche. A coach, on the other hand, is usually paid to help you uncover the answers within you, and may provide tools and exercises to help the discovery process.

You can easily drive someone away if they sense you're asking for a huge time commitment. Start by asking to take them out for coffee or lunch. The agenda is simply to meet and learn how you can help each other.

If you do establish an ongoing relationship, be sure to nurture it. Let your mentor drive the length of the meetings and the agenda because they are giving you the value of their time. In your meetings, be open to a new perspective and willing to listen. Stay in regular contact with them and keep them up to date on what you are doing.

You'll probably be surprised at the number of successful people who are open to being a mentor. As people climb the ladder of success and significance, they're often looking to turn around and see whom they might be able to help.

The mentor I have actually found me; we were introduced through a mutual friend. He is an attorney, and he knew that I was working on a new venture and that the contracts were critical; he recognized that it was important for me to be sure my interests were protected, so he offered to look at it from the outside, with his attorney's eye.

The fact that he said, "Let me mentor you and let me help you" absolutely bowled me over, because I wasn't looking at the time. When we meet, we talk about what's going on in both of our businesses. He's adding value to me, and in return, I try to give value back by making connections for him and his business. It's been mutually beneficial for both of us.

> *One aspect of serendipity to bear in mind is that you have to be looking for something in order to find something else.*

-Lawrence Block

Making Connections That Count

I know that great connections can happen anytime and anywhere. Where have you made the most interesting connections? Here are some ways you can make more and better connections.

Put yourself in the right place. Location, location, location isn't just for real estate. If you want to bump into people who are relevant to what you want to achieve, put yourself in the middle. Is there a professional organization, networking group, or even a co-working space that would increase your collision rate? What about social media?

Show up with intention. Making connections starts with your intention. Pay attention to what you're thinking before heading out to your next meeting or networking event.

Be fantastic at making introductions. If you want to speed up your serendipity rate, then start making more introductions. Be the connector!

Follow up. You can do all of the above, but it won't matter if you don't follow up and follow through.

> *You can get everything in life you want if you will just help enough other people get what they want.*

-Zig Ziglar

Serendipitous Encounters

Tony Hsieh, CEO of Zappos, talks about the importance of increasing your collision rate, or your interaction with other people, in order to have more serendipitous encounters. Such encounters can connect you with new people and new ideas, and maybe even inspire your next leap. Your RAS can speed up your number of serendipitous encounters. When you know what you're looking for, the right people will appear. Making connections starts with your intention. Pay attention to what you're thinking before heading out for the day.

Fantastic connections can happen anytime and anywhere!

Here's the story of a connection I made that led to one of my own serendipitous encounters. For years, I've been a huge fan of Bob Burg, author of business books such as *Endless Referrals, The Go-Giver, Go-Givers Sell More,* and *It's Not about You.* He's known as the ultimate connector, and he is my networking idol. You could call him the Peyton Manning of networking. He has an impressive circle of influence and hangs with thought leaders like John Maxwell and Randy Gage. Years ago, when I didn't have a clue how to network, I remember sitting in an audience of 8,000 people at a conference, and Bob was giving the keynote. I was just in awe.

Later, when I was making the shift from wallflower to connector, I decided to send Bob a direct message via Twitter because I was doing a talk on networking and mindset for a local leadership organization and I wanted to get his perspective. I thought, "Why not ask; the worst he could say is no." I was surprised to get a response from Bob within 15 minutes that said, "Absolutely! I'm happy to talk to you." He sent me his email address and said, "Email me your questions." I sent the questions back and then he replied, "Great! I want to talk to you via phone." When we had the conversation (which was fantastic), Bob told me he was going to be in Kansas City the following week, which I had somehow missed on Twitter.

The next week in Kansas City, Bob spoke to an intimate group of about 30 people. We had a conversation afterward and started developing a relationship. A couple of years later, I invited Bob to Kansas City to speak. At that event I had the privilege of sharing the stage with Bob and making several key introductions for him.

It took courage to reach out to Bob via Twitter to ask for his insights. He could have said no, or he could have chosen not to reply at all. But it turns out that Bob is extraordinarily gracious, and I never would have known that if I hadn't taken the leap to contact him.

Remember, you are truly six degrees (or less) of separation away from anyone you want to meet. So think bigger. Reach out and ask. It's okay. You'll be surprised. Connect to those people who can add a lot to your life, and, just as important, you can add to theirs.

Shallow men believe in luck or in circumstance. Strong men believe in cause and effect.

- Ralph Waldo Emerson

Nine

The Net Will Appear

❝ *Keep your dreams alive. Understand to achieve anything requires faith and belief in yourself, vision, hard work, determination, and dedication. Remember all things are possible for those who believe.* **❞**

-Gail Devers

It's important to have a plan and a process, set goals, and shift your self-talk, but belief is the most powerful element. If you believe anything is possible, it's easier to take the leap and trust that the net will appear.

The Power of Belief

One of my favorite books is *The Biology of Belief* by Dr. Bruce Lipton. It is a fascinating read on the study of epigenetics. In layman's terms, epigenetics is about how all the cells in your body are affected by your thoughts. Dr. Lipton's research shows that our genes and DNA do not control our biology; instead, our DNA is controlled by signals from outside the cell, including energetic messages that come from our positive and negative thoughts.

In his book, Dr. Lipton shares a study that's extraordinarily powerful. In 2002, the Baylor School of Medicine published a study in the *New England Journal of Medicine*. They were looking at patients with debilitating knee pain, and they wanted to know which kind of surgery gave patients the greatest relief. So they separated the patients into three groups. They shaved the damaged cartilage of the patients in the first group; they flushed out the knee joints of those in the second group; and the people in the third group were only made to think they had surgery: The patients were sedated, incisions were made, and the team talked and acted just like they were doing the entire surgical process, even down to the knee-washing procedure. They also spent the same amount of time in the operating room.

The groups that had surgery absolutely got the results they were looking for.

But the placebo group improved just as much, without surgery!

If your thoughts are powerful enough to affect the pain of arthritis in your knees, how are they affecting the rest of your life?

❝Ordinary people believe only in the possible. Extraordinary people visualize not what is possible or probable, but rather what is impossible. And by visualizing the impossible, they begin to see it as possible.❞

-Cherie Carter-Scott

Ordinary People Can Do the Impossible

As I was doing research on innovative people, companies, and products, I found a story about Richard Van As, who accidentally cut off his fingers while he was doing woodworking at his house in South Africa.

While he was in the hospital, he decided that he was going to figure out a way to make a set of fingers for himself, because they told him that it was going to cost $10,000 for a prosthetic hand.

When he shared his idea, the people around him kept telling him how impossible it was. But the more they told him that, the more determined he was to make it happen.

Richard started doing research and couldn't find anything close to what he had in his mind. But, on YouTube, he found a video by a guy in the U.S. named Ivan Owen who had built giant mechanical puppet hands.

After Richard saw this video, he contacted Ivan, and they started exchanging ideas. Ivan was the first one who told Richard, "I believe we can make this happen."

Using 3D printers gave them the ability to make prototypes very inexpensively, and they could both do it; that way, they had the same parts at the same time. Sending plans back and forth and working together, it took them about a year to come up with the final product.

Richard started with this idea to solve his immediate need, but as they moved forward, both men realized how many people, and especially children, around the world could benefit from their work. They put the design and instructions on the Internet for free, and now, with the materials and a 3D printer, anybody can create a robohand for less than a $150—and people are already doing just that.

Mason, a 16-year-old in Louisburg, Kansas, who had befriended a nine-year-old boy who was born without some of the fingers on his hand, used Richard and Ivan's plans and the 3D printer at the Johnson County Library to build a robohand for his friend.

It's one of those serendipitous moments. It started off with Richard's desire to create his own prosthetic hand and his unstoppable belief, but it expanded to have a greater impact in the world.

> **We can't be afraid of change. You may feel very secure in the pond that you are in, but if you never venture out of it, you will never know that there is such a thing as an ocean, a sea. Holding onto something that is good for you now may be the very reason why you don't have something better.**
>
> -C. JoyBell C.

Trust the Process

Change can be hard. If it were easy, everyone would be doing it. Change is also a choice. Your subconscious mind creates comfort zones based on what's happened to you in the past. The key to moving through change is to be aware of what comfort zones could be limiting you instead of just keeping you safe. When you learn to intentionally push comfort zones, you'll begin to see change as an adventure.

Even if you can't see exactly where you're going or don't have all the resources you need, just keep moving along; that's the most important thing. Believe the net will appear. The people, the resources, the information will show up right when you need it, as long as you're moving in the right direction. You know what you need to know, and you can build the plane while you're flying it. You don't have to have all the details, but be sure you're on the lookout for the opportunities.

I had this experience with my speaking career. Seeing people speak lit my desire to pursue it as a business. I would shake when I held a microphone, but eventually I just threw myself out there. When someone asked, I told her I was a speaker even though I wasn't, and then she asked for a video, which had not been produced because I wasn't a speaker, so I had to put together a video. But once I started going down that path, the right people showed up. Darren LaCroix just happened to come to Kansas City to speak for the local National Speakers Association chapter, and I just happened to be going, and Darren ended up becoming my speaking coach. Then, fast forward to speaking at TEDxUMKC in 2013, which led to me writing this book (a huge leap!).

In the words of Dallas Cowboys coach Jimmy Johnson, "Do you want to be safe and good, or do you want to take a chance and be great? It's important to trust the process, but you also have to take action to be great. Don't let fear keep you stuck. A lot of times, fears keep us stuck because we believe we're not good enough or we don't have the skill set. But you can learn the skill set; you can get out there and acquire the knowledge to be good enough.

Don't confuse what you believe with what you know.

Don't let subconscious beliefs get in the way. The stories we tell ourselves are setting us up for failure, not success.

When we get stuck in fear and limiting thoughts, we also give up our personal power.

Here are some signs that you might be giving away your personal power:
- You wait for directions
- You don't set any goals (if you have no direction, that is just where you will be: nowhere)
- You have trouble focusing—you try one thing but then give up and move to another before giving yourself ample time to be proficient
- You resist change

If you are waiting for the world to bring you a winning lottery ticket to life, it's going to be a long wait. Successful people set goals and take steps to ensure their success, including leaps.

> *I have found that helping people to develop personal goals has proven to be the most effective way to help them cope with problems. Observing the lives of people who have mastered adversity, I have noted that they have established goals and sought with all their effort to achieve them. From the moment they decided to concentrate all their energies on a specific objective, they began to surmount the most difficult odds.*
>
> **-Ari Kiev**

If you're stuck, start by identifying a few areas where you've seen little to no behavioral change despite your best efforts—for example, you've tried blocking out whole days for big projects or going to the gym first thing in the morning, but instead you waste time surfing the Internet or on social media and nothing's changing. Then zoom out to determine your real goal. Why was this activity important to you in the first place? Maybe you wanted to feel like you're finishing priority tasks, or have a healthier, more physically active life.

Now brainstorm other tactics you could use to achieve those goals. If you've never managed to block out an entire day for your major projects, try finding two half-days instead. If you hate the gym or aren't a morning person, don't expect yourself to go there first thing in the morning! Instead, consider options like a bike ride after work or exercises you can do at home before bed. Identify activities that align with your natural tendencies.

> *You need a plan to build a house. To build a life, it is even more important to have a plan or goal.*
>
> **-Zig Ziglar**

Your Brain on Goals

Where do you want to be in one year, five years, and ten years? Have you thought about it or do you actually have a plan/goals written out? If you don't set goals, you'll just be floating around. Your energy and time may be spent on activities that play no role in the larger vision for your life—and you won't be aware of it because you're just living life as it is.

The brain only gets super focused if and when it needs to; otherwise, just like a computer, one could argue that it goes to sleep and does the minimal amount of work needed. When a person has no clear goals, doesn't write their goals down, and doesn't have plans to achieve those goals, their level of goal arousal, passion, and overall enthusiasm is low. As a result, they do not recognize or identify the people, opportunities, situations or resources that could be helpful to them.

Setting goals gives you clarity on what you really want. Goals give you focus and internal motivation and keep you accountable. When you write down your goals, you are choosing a specific direction or destination that is important for you, as well as the specific steps to get there. You focus on what matters.

Another key element of goals is that they make you uncomfortable with where you are currently. It's kind of like deliberately creating a problem for yourself, so your subconscious goes to work to find ways to solve it.

Setting a goal is a conscious decision that you want to change something. It's the difference between living intentionally and living by accident.

This is where the rubber meets the road, so to speak. You'll find out where your comfort zones are, and now that you've read this book, you're better equipped to push through them. Remember, when you set a goal and continuously visualize the end result, this creates the drive and energy to change reality so that it matches the picture you have been visualizing.

As I said, the great thing about goals is that they give you a target, like the top of the hill when I was on my bike, so you know where you're going. But if you're not careful you'll run into problems like I did, when I stayed focused on the top of the hill instead of just over my handlebars. The dilemma with huge goals is that your brain doesn't see anything bigger than what it can accomplish within 24 hours; it declares BS on everything that takes longer than that. So say you want to lose 50 pounds. Your BS monitor will say, "Okay, but I can't lose that much in 24 hours" and will just want to keep you in your comfort zone instead. You can lose an eighth of a pound in 24 hours, though, so you should start with small changes—go for a walk, cut 100 calories—so the brain will just focus on the immediate goal without getting overwhelmed looking at the big picture.

If you had to clean out your garage piled to the ceiling with boxes and junk, it could feel overwhelming. In this instance, don't even look at 24 hours, but just what you can accomplish in five minutes. Just move one box, then the next, and then the next. Do the same thing with taking leaps. Start small, and as you achieve those small goals (and celebrate your wins), you'll have more motivation to set bigger goals.

You'll never know what you can accomplish unless you start. And you might be surprised at the results.

> **“If you set goals and go after them with all the determination you can muster, your gifts will take you places that will amaze you.”**
>
> -Les Brown

LBs and NTs

When we're trying to take a leap, no matter how big or how small, fear gets in the way. We have that hesitancy and uncertainty; that internal dialogue starts going, and we wonder if we're doing the right thing.

You've probably had times when someone else has said something that helped propel you forward to take the leap. How can you do the same and help others take their own leaps? Start paying attention to how you talk to the people around you. Are you focusing on what their strengths are, what their capabilities are?

When you see that desire in somebody to make a change, and you see the right attitude and you know that they can figure it out, are you coaching them towards success or are you talking them out of it and saying, "You better play it safe"? Point them in the right direction. Help them see what they can't yet see for themselves. Look for ways you can pay it forward and truly impact someone else's life.

Great leaders not only inspire leaps, they take the first leap!

They clearly tell the vision of the company and coach their team towards success. The very best leaders help their teams to believe in themselves—they inspire them to do more than they think they can, to entertain possibilities that stretch the limits of their beliefs.

Another powerful tool to help yourself or others move forward is LBs and NTs, which stands for "liked best" and "next time." To use this, ask yourself or someone else:

- What did you like best about what you did?
- What are you doing right?
- Where are the strengths?
- Where have you seen the biggest growth?
- Would you do anything differently the next time?

At the end, instead of "you're not doing this," or "you're not doing this well," shift it to "next time." What can you do next time to get the results that you want? What can you do next time to improve yourself or elevate your performance?

You can use this for yourself, and with your family, your friends, and especially your children. A great thing to ask your kids at the end of the day is, "What did you like best about today? What was the one thing that stood out? What are you looking forward to tomorrow?" These questions help them to use their imagination and get them looking for the good stuff.

It's important to pay attention to what you're focusing on (is it the alligators or the good stuff?) and what you're saying about it. Remember the power of the negativity bias? Once you start looking for the things that are going right, you're going to see more that's right. Once you start looking for opportunities, you're going to see more opportunities.

> **"A real decision is measured by the fact that you've taken a new action. If there's no action, you haven't truly decided."**
>
> ~Tony Robbins

Ready, Set, Leap!

It doesn't matter if it's small or large; take the leap. And when it comes to business and companies, this is especially important, because if you don't take the leap, innovation is going to leave you in the dust.

At the end of my TEDx talk, I say that sometimes, a leap is into a pool, and other times, it's off a mountain. You'll need to decide which leaps you need to take immediately, and whether they should be big leaps or small ones. Either way, you'll never know what's truly possible in your life or business until you're willing to take that first leap.

Now think about the shift you want to make. Is it something personal? Something professional? Is it really obvious what shift you need to make, or is it just that something's not settled and it's kind of nudging inside of you? If you're not sure, just sit back and listen to your inner guidance. But, ultimately, just go for it. Commit to what matters. Know there's going to be a little discomfort in change, but choose to focus on the positive payoff. You're drawn toward what you think about, so think about what you want your life to look like one year, five years, and ten years from now (not to mention when you're 80 years old), after you've taken the leap.

Once you start down that road with the right mindset, I promise that you are going to be surprised and thrilled with the opportunities that come your way and the people that come into your life.

LEAP EXERCISE ▬▬▬▬▬▬▬▬▬▬▬▬▬▬▬

Design Your Perfect Year

Imagine that it is one year from today. What has to happen for you to be happy about the progress you have made in your business and life over the next 12 months? Ask yourself, what would make your year perfect? What do you want to keep, add, change, redo, evolve, be, have, become, do, offer, fix, solve, provide, improve, initiate, learn, accomplish, continue, and experience in the coming year? Include elements that are already working perfectly and those that you want to add or change.

> *Destiny is not a matter of chance; it is a matter of choice. It is not a thing to be waited for; it is a thing to be achieved.*

-William Jennings Bryan

I have done my best to give you the Layman's Guide you need to get from there to here. The tools and concepts shared in this book have worked for me and for others, and can work for you as well. But this is where the information and inspiration stop. Know that the greatest power—your willingness and determination—is inside you. Start by letting go of excuses. Believe. Get busy doing what you can, with what you've got, from where you are. Start now. Enjoy the journey. And finally, remember that once you're here, you'll always have another there. So I challenge you to just take another leap!

> *Life belongs to those who believe in the beauty of their dreams.*

-Eleanor Roosevelt

REFERENCES

1. Introduction
Harvard Business School
http://www.hbs.edu/faculty/Publication%20Files/12-035_a3c1f5d8-452d-4b48-9a49-812424424cc2.pdf

2. Chapter 2
Kyle Maynard
http://en.wikipedia.org/wiki/Kyle_Maynard

3. Chapter 2
Nikki Stone
http://nikkistone.com/speaker-intros.htm

4. Chapter 7
Kia Commercial
http://www.youtube.com/watch?v=HYIYXRR95Ak

28183916R00057

Made in the USA
Middletown, DE
05 January 2016